In the Key of Love

POPS the Club Anthology V
Stories, Poems and Artwork

POPS
THE CLUB

In the Key of Love: POPS the Club Anthology V
Stories, Poems and Artwork
© 2018 POPS the Club

Editors: Amy Friedman, Dennis Danziger, Lynette Padwa, Kate Zentall
Copyediting and Proofreading: Sonia Faye, Claire Lazebnik,
Natalie Lima, & Matthew Tester
Design by Monica Thomas, TLC Book Design, *www.TLCBookDesign.com*

Cover photograph © 2018 Ellie Perez Sanchez

Interior cover © 2018 Kennedy King

POPS the Club logo by Kenny Barela

ISBN 978-0-9988382-0-5 (paperback)
ISBN 978-0-9988382-1-2 (ebook)

Visit our website www.POPStheClub.com

Embrace by Kennedy King

The strongest love is the love that
can demonstrate its fragility.

Paulo Coehlo

Table of Contents

Part 1: Cracked Masks-17

Part 2: We the Brave-37

Part 3: Who We Are and Where We Are From—69

Table of Contents

Part 4: Understand Us—101

Part 5: Mothers and Fathers–121

Part 6: Heartbreak–147

Table of Contents

Part 7: Looking Back-175

Part 8: Six Word Memoirs-187

Part 9: See Our Stories–191

Introduction

by Amy Friedman

On February 13, 2018, Pops the Club celebrated our fifth anniversary. As I stood in the classroom at Venice High where it all began, I looked around at the 40-plus students eating salad and lasagna, at the five volunteers serving food, at the lead teacher and the four other teachers chatting with students, and I couldn't help but remember what our first meetings were like. Back then it was just me and my husband, a teacher, ten students, peanut butter and jelly sandwiches, and quiet conversations about the way we felt about having loved ones in prison, jail, detention or deported. I remembered listening to those young men and women struggling to find the words to express emotions they had buried, looking for ways to talk about the secrets they had kept—the grief they'd felt, the shame, the way they had been stigmatized. They talked about brothers, cousins, fathers, mothers, sisters lost to the system. Sometimes they cried. Sometimes they raged. Sometimes they confessed. Sometimes they complained. They applauded speakers who came to share their own experiences and praised the volunteers who, over those first months, began to trickle in to help. They fell in love, with each other and with their own strength and resilience. And as we watched and listened, we understood that POPS was needed in schools across the city, and across the country.

As of January 2018, we have POPS clubs in eight schools in Los Angeles—Belmont, Culver City, El Camino Real Charter, James Monroe, LA High School for the Arts, Lawndale, Santa Monica and Venice High. We're at Carver and Mays High Schools in Atlanta and in Harrisburg, Pennsylvania at Sci Tech and Steelton Highspire. We're in Baltimore at Renaissance High. Soon there will be POPS clubs in the Bronx, in Long Island City, and in San Francisco. Each week we field calls from students, teachers, social workers, police officers, parents, lawyers, and judges everywhere who understand the importance of recognizing this population so long overlooked. We're working to launch as many clubs as we can.

With this, our fifth anthology, we offer a sampling of the words and wisdom of these young people who possess knowledge they wish to share, not only with those who don't understand the real impact of mass incarceration but also with their loved ones inside who too often aren't aware of the toll their sentences take on their loved ones.

With the launch of each new club, with each new POPS student, with each graduate (many of whom now volunteer), I feel more honored to have the opportunity to absorb their understanding, imagination, and generosity. No one says it better than AP English teacher Hazel Kight Witham who teaches at Venice High and comes nearly every week to the POPS meeting there—the POPS meeting her husband, teacher Drake Witham, sponsors. At our birthday party, Hazel offered up this poem, the perfect opening for *In the Key of Love.*

Ode to POPS,
on the occasion of its fifth birthday

by Hazel Kight Witham

Four and one-half years ago
on my first day at Venice High

DJ Danziger went and made me cry

mixing the story of ya'll and your folks, ya'll—young folks
breaking free of the pain
of our criminal injustice system of shame

the one we've constructed on this unjust foundation
the cracked bedrock of this broke-from-the-get-go nation

See, I thought I knew something of my own
small prisons, tiny cages

but I did not know how far the real bars reached

till DJ Danziger and MC Friedman
showed up with your hard-carved words, and preached

and I watched, how those two slung prompts and promises
and ya'll spit bars about bars

crafting lines about climbing up from the
heartache of loved ones lost and hard things past

and so for me, POPS became the place to be
every Wednesday, first in 120 then later in 1-3-7

where some new guy showed up to fill big shoes

But the constant, beyond DJs and MCs and new guys and guest
spots has always, always, been you

you, ya'll who show up, carrying the silent stories
of those we've forsaken, those we've forgot

but ya'll—you all—you have not

you've resurrected them for us in
your words, your lines, your stories
reaching across all that time

served
in your words you serve those serving time,
you bond with each other in the serving line,
sit and break bread,
spin your words
break bars, break silence,
break ignorance,

break me,

how ya'll have broken me,
week after week,
shattered me
into smallest pieces
so I may come back together
stronger, wiser,
somehow more whole

piece by piece,
and isn't that how peace is built?
peace upon peace?

because since you've splintered me,
shaken me,
made me understand,
that ya'll, that them,
that really
I, You All, and Them,

we are all Us.

we are all in these prisons, these cages,
small and vast,
and we all must get each other

out.
together.

Drawing by Mya Edwards

∽◡ Part 1 ◡∼

Cracked Masks

Only when we are brave enough to explore the darkness
will we discover the infinite power of the light.

Brené Brown

Évolution

by Daniel Ortiz

Nothing stays the same
One day to another everyone will start to change
Friends and family will start to fade
No one remains straight, like a bullet's range
I've got hate from brothers from my own gang
It hurts because it's my family who say I be acting strange
That I'm a bitch for leaving the game

It's not that. It's cause I wanna live and act my
Damn age
I know I might never rap on stage
But it's talent that I earned and locked in a cage
I might never be rich, but money Ima have to obtain

As for the gang, I have it in my heart and it will forever remain
The love I got for 8lest is strong, I can't even explain
'Cause the same gang runs through our veins
Even though he tells me I'm a piece of sh-- and a disgrace
But I've learned to use my brain
And stop using drugs as a form to entertain
They've damaged my teeth, leaving permanent stains
When I brush I see my blood go down the drain

I sit back and see the world as a damaged place
Through my eyes I can see nothing but grey

Cracked Masks

But my melody I have to regain
In my short 16 years I learned evolution is true
At one point you don't know who's who
And especially who are you
It happened to me I've changed my views
Contemplating all the garbage I've got myself into
And the struggle I went through
And how my life has expired tags that I need to renew
Sometimes I go back in time to review
How lousy I dressed in all navy blue
Till today my dreams I don't think I can pursue

I need God or someone to give me a clue
Of what the f--- I'm supposed to do
'Cause my old friends are covered in tattoos
Their eyes bloody red as if drenched in shampoo
Inhaling NOS out of a colored balloon

I see my life like an unfinished work of art
I say this coming from my heart
Many make fun and say, "you're fixing your life, do you even
    know where to start?"
Most say that I'm retarded, I've never been called smart
That's why I'm going to school so I can change
'Cause in life there's always a restart

Most don't know what I want
I don't need girls, cars or drugs
I want education, don't matter the cost
It's been months that I'm called soft or a 187 mark
I'm told if I make it Ima forget about the hood
I will never forget my past—it built my character

So I'm out here taking nine classes, catching up on every semester
Everything I learn I save like a collector
I only roll with the real, the fake got me peeping like a smoke
    detector
I want you to feel my feelings because my words are a projector
Reason I talk at POPS is respect to Danziger, my mentor
I lived the thug life and already paid the price
I lost a couple brothers to a bag of ice
Not once but more than twice
It's a huge number so I can't say precise

And it's true, just ask the government hearing me through my
    device
I'm lucky to be alive in the sunlight
It's all because of God and Jesus Christ
I'm going through life as a blue shining knight
'Cause in the streets you go in raw, bullets cook you up and your
    blood turns into lard
Me and society are playing poker, but I hold my last card
'Cause I've lost all my chips to society, but I feel like I've been
    robbed
At this moment in my life I'm going thru evolution
The stress be killing me so I write as a form of solution

I'm turning my direction 'cause heaven is where I wanna go
It's the only institution
I'm fighting to survive in the bullet debris pollution
'Cause all my life has been an illusion
But I'm almost done, I can see the conclusion
I'm end my life in battle in the black and brown against the
    white supremacist revolution

Maybe One Day

by Amy Medina

She had a history.

She's been living on earth for 16 years. She's never liked her chaotic life—family members, including her grandpa and friends dying one after another. She could never get used to it.

Now she hates passing by cemeteries. Her heartaches when she sees families going through what she's been through.

She's been living a nightmare. No room for dreams and fantasies because they seem beyond far away, impossible.

She realized at a young age that nobody is forever, so she didn't let herself get too close to anyone. Every morning, while brushing her teeth, she reminds herself of this truth. So she distances herself from others. She flies solo.

Often she thinks of her grandpa who died and took her heart with him. Pain seems to be all that she can feel.

She's staring at two paths. She doesn't know which one to choose. Left or right. Bad or good. Just choose! But she doesn't. She's confused. So, she keeps her head low. Walks with her chin down. One day maybe, just maybe one day she'll choose. But for now she fakes every smile, doesn't want anyone to wonder why she's crying.

She had a history. One too painful to think about. Too hard to handle.

Maybe her history will have another chapter.

And hopefully that chapter will be good.

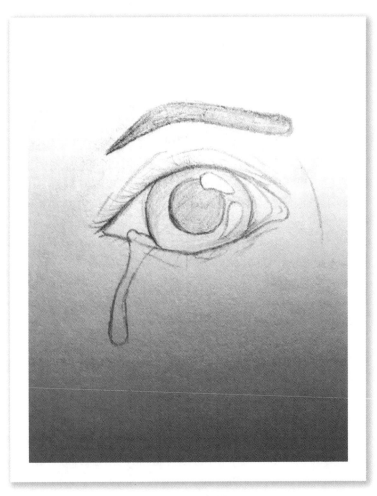

Tears by Kennedy King

Mistakes

by Angela Gomez

In my life I felt I've been a mistake
Nothing seems right or goes my way
I feel like I'm a burden and should be carried away.
All I want to do is run from those who hurt me
From those who misunderstood me
From those who wanted more than I can give.
I was torn to pieces by those I loved
As I heard about my father's arrest
All remaining strength went down the drain.
Yes, he wasn't perfect, but he tried his best for me
unlike any other.
As I could no longer handle the pain, I spotted the
blade that could slowly end my suffering.
One after another, I finally felt free
I saw the red flowing from me
I was no longer broken because I'd found my way
To a solution.
They all thought I was perfect but not everyone is
as fine as they seem.
We are all broken at some point, but the choice is
yours if you want to show it.
This is my story of how I came to be.

What I Learned

by Brian Hernandez

When someone in the family goes to prison, it doesn't affect just the inmate, it affects the whole family. Many people look at incarceration as a man or woman going behind bars, but the story goes deeper than that. When a father or mother is behind bars, the children lose a person who provides for them. Sadly, this can lead to children going into foster care and struggling with poverty. The loss of a parent figure can take a toll on children and lead them to act out in school, to be unfocused, to feel lost. It's hard for anyone to see a loved one behind bars and talk to them behind a glass wall.

Growing up, I saw this hardship in my brother's friend when his dad was incarcerated and then deported. I saw a young kid grow up with no dad, saw him living in a one-bedroom apartment with his mom and his sister because they couldn't afford a bigger place. He used to have to talk to his dad through a glass wall over over the phone. He was just a young kid, but I saw that he had to grow up fast and had to help his mom. I remember him walking home from school after having to help his mom with work. He had to wear the same pair of shoes year round.

I remember he wore the biggest smile and he taught me not to take anything for granted. He taught me to always be happy for what I have because some have it harder than you think. He taught me never to bring anyone down.

Meeting him changed my life because growing up I took my father for granted. Watching him growing up with no dad helped me realize that the absence of a parent impacts life in many ways.

I stopped taking my family for granted. I learned from him that life is beautiful, and it's a blessing to love everyone around you.

The Weight of My Pain

by Crystal Gonzalez

The weight of my pain is all on my neck
the noose is tightening slower, now all I'm thinking is death
My tears are running out. What do I got left?
Like I'm losing touch with my soul
Haven't been knowing where to go.
Do you see the soul that cries through smiles?
Or the skin that tells stories through cuts?
I'm that kid who people just don't give a f---
Pause my pain as I roll my blunt
Grab my mind cuz I'm having thoughts I can't cope with,
    they're eating me up
But I don't show weakness so I stay
    like a clown
They say I'm here for a reason
But what's that reason for?
Sometimes I feel like I haven't even
    opened that door

Ink Stain

by Isabella Balbi

Once I was a molten blob of ash and acid, a toxic shell of a human being. My shyness consumed me, my self-hatred grew in my chest like a rotten crop, and my depression loomed over me so severely I knew that what I was feeling had to be more than typical teen angst. I bottled it. For years. For my mother, who despite countless hours of overtime and saved paychecks, could not afford to muster up money for anything besides rent and the water bill, let alone for pills and sessions she wouldn't understand my need for. For my father, who'd look at me in shame and insist that other people have it worse, who never understood that these words of criticism were only contributing to the problem. And for myself. For my thoughts of self-doubt and the internalized social stigma that comes along with this mental illness. The loneliness, fear, and sadness stuck in my chest like a thick tar, poisoning me from the inside out.

The only antidote to make it spill out of me was writing. I thank the heavens every day for giving me the words to express the conflicts within me, for giving me some way to spew out the nebulas and black holes in my heart. Pages upon pages splattered with ink blotches and twisted letters were better than any bottle of Prozac, because they acknowledged the pain as a voice, and I discovered that writing until your hand aches and your eyes blur is okay, because it means you have something to say.

Through time I have learned to be happy again, to find solace in friendships that are deeper bonds than the ones I have through blood, and in the simple acts of kindness I find in the world around me. When I see a father reading to his daughter, or a teenager assisting an elderly couple, I feel my heart swell with the love I am missing out on at home. I cope, and I feel content, because my perspective has drastically changed, although my situation has stayed the same.

Into the Void by Kyra Hill

Malaki

by Milena Mousli

I wonder if he stood on the ledge or let his legs dangle.
I wonder if he pushed himself off or if he bent his legs and
    jumped.
I wonder what his apartment looked like.
I wonder what the window looked like.
I wonder what sounds his body made hitting the cement.
I wonder what the autopsy was.
I wonder how many bones he broke.
I wonder what truly killed him, a skull fracture, internal
    bleeding, ribs shattered.
I wish I knew.

First Time

by Nicole Scott

First time hearing from you after three years was entertaining,
    enticing.
First time seeing you after three years was exciting.
First time smelling you and touching you after three whole years
We embraced for so long I forgot three years had passed.
First time tasting you after that only felt right.

My Flaws to My Beauty

by Jessica De La Mora

I love you, all of you. From your flaws to your beauty, your
    laughter to your tears.
I need to learn how to love myself.
It's hard when you are surrounded by beautiful people and you
    feel so imperfect,
When all you want to be is perfect.
Okay, we all know perfection is not real,
But every time I look into the mirror at my reflection, I hurt.
I feel it dramatically in my very own heart.
It's hard to explain the feeling I have when I look down at my
    body.
I feel as if my stomach is just twisted.
I feel sick and a pain in my heart.
I instantly start to feel sorrow.
It hurts to look down at my body and not be able to smile, only cry.
Hardest part of it all, this is a daily routine.
Getting in and out of the shower or passing by a mirror or glass
    window,
Everyone thinks I'm checking myself out.
If they only knew all I am doing is judging my body and my
    flaws.

Untitled by Kennedy King

She Comes to Revisit

by John Rodriguez

I walk and she peers at me, not wanting to be seen. Shy, of course. I haven't seen her in some time, and she's interested in how I've grown up, how I've managed. I normally am cautious. Mother warned about strangers.

I walk and there she is, at my peripherals, off in the distance and in the angles of my quickest movements. She doesn't like to be seen.

I get goosebumps inside. My prickly hide is stunned as she veers near, skin still soft, glowing. Wavy hair of the Greeks touched her, blessed her, and gave her this thing that she could walk in, but to most she is not there. I know I shouldn't but I invite her in.

Her eyes know me—big, brown, studying. I slowly sit in the middle of the parking lot, my hands not connecting to the ground. Finally, she pulls away from behind the white wall in the driveway and takes tiny footsteps toward me.

Nervously, face hidden within golden waves, she points her chin to the pavement and smiles. I do too. My eyes are shut, but I can sense her every gesture. She's quiet. Her feet circle me, and I continue to look down, eyelashes from both lids closely pressed together.

She sits in front of me. I have not seen her in years and each of her features has changed, but youth still resonates within her. Slowly, with an unknown softness, she touches my fingertips from beneath my palm and curls my fingers with hers.

She listens, and we converse. Not with words. I know how she's been, and certainly she knows me. She knows I hurt and love, that I'm trying to figure things out, that the world is tough, and like a mother she seems to understand. She smiles, and it makes me feel better already.

Hours have passed, and I know that she's gone. The lady who will revisit me in some years is actually pleasant. She will not waste her time telling me of her dominance or strength. I sit there pasted to the concrete, and in the distance, I hear her whisper that today is not my turn.

Courthouses

by Ireland Neville

The endless row of marble floors
Marble white as snow
Marble that could construct
A modern Parthenon
Yet gone to waste on a floor
A far cry from "A Wonder of The World"

In a building, priceless
To those who don't go inside
Amazing history
To those who didn't write it
A reminder of our country's democracy
But the last place you will find freedom

Liberty and Justice for All
The golden letters read
And underneath them
Men in expensive suits
File lawsuits
For those who don't have money
To suit them

Silk ties with
Colors like tie dye
Tie their knots
With those who

Don't have money to
Tide them over

Ivory buttons
Shuffle into a wooden elevator
As rough fingers push buttons
Calloused fingers who could
Open doors to safety
But in

Stead stay
Confined

Where truth prevails
At an hourly rate
Where public servants
Are slave-owners themselves
Where rulings are fair
At an unfair price
Where agreements are made
To make money

Lawyers, judges, and secretaries
All corrupted under this system
Judicial
Root word for equity in Latin
Equity as in wealth?
I cannot tell

~ Part 2 ~

We the Brave

I saw that my life was a vast glowing empty page
and I could do anything I wanted.

Jack Kerouac

Sunset by Ellie Perez Sanchez

Legacy
by Kei'Arri McGruder

As I walk down the street I see all these eyes on me as if I'm nothing but a lowdown dirty criminal

The white lady clenches her purse, making my head go lower and lower, knowing that she sees me as a danger

How can a black man be so ashamed of something he should praised being with open hands?

Each and every day, I fight back against the guns, drugs, temptations of girls I would love to ummmm …but I don't budge

Can't even wear the wrong color knowing a young dark-skinned brother might mistake me for another

Then pow, shoot me dead and yet again another dead son for an unfortunate mother

It happens so often. That's why I have to stay cautious

Not trying to be a baby daddy at 16, shi__, please, does it look like I want some kids? Nah, bro, not me

Or even jail before I hit 18. They will not take my dignity away from me behind bars. I won't let that happen to me

But because I am me, people only see what they wanna see

Not the true me but the painted picture of a young black man the way they think I'm supposed to be

Have to keep my hands in my pants walking into the store not trying to have the security follow me around anymore

They expect me to exceed in sports like football or on the courts

Not in academics, like math or physics

I'm expected to underachieve, to not succeed

Because I'm a shade too dark to be smart

They think we all bang, talk in slang, dress with our pants past our waists and have no home training

And when they ask my mom's name, ha, they expect me to say Quanisha, Bonquesha, Kisha

Names they think are common for all black queens

Just another stereotype, because it seems as though if her name ends in such a sound—sha or quee—

She's just another ghetto lady with a messed-up weave and 20 kids who don't even know their own daddy

And gen American expects me to turn out to become a deadbeat, but nah, not me

I'm breaking these boundaries

Creating a man out of me, someone America doesn't wanna see

They will try to break me, shake me, and maybe even beat me, but I will prosper
and
become a legacy

My Body is Beautiful

by Kayla Armstrong

My body is beautiful, no matter if I'm skinny, fat, or curvy, I love my body. My body was made from the roots of the flowers that start to bloom in June and July, and I can see why my body catches a lot of men's eyes. My body was designed by the gods in the sky, but who would know that evil was preying on me and wanted to see me cry.

The golden temple that was mine full of gold, jewelry, and the sacred, where my words were my spells, my actions were rituals, but my temple was broken into by an individual. The individual who broke into my temple was famished for lust. Body shattered, feeling as if my life was at the top and I'm at the bottom of the ladder. Temple destroyed, the roots of the flowers weren't growing and the spells coming out my mouth were croaking. Wondering why the individual did this, wasn't he supposed to love me?

As a stepfather he repeatedly, illegally, and secretly broke into my temple, and I said spells to free myself and cast him back to the cell he came from, and he will never be set free.

My body is beautiful, no matter if I'm skinny, fat, or curvy, no matter if my temple is broken into and will never be the same before it was broken into, my body is beautiful.

My body is beautiful because it is a flower. It makes sure that no matter who pulls it out of the ground, it will grow back. My body was broken, but my spirit is not and negativity tried so hard to pull me into the dark, but it will not.

Who Am I?

by Amyas Njoku

Who am I really?
A question I constantly ask myself
A question I am unsure how to answer
A question I'm always looking for an answer to
Trying to find myself
Always a struggle
Never finding the answer
Trying to be myself and not knowing who that is
Not knowing who I want to be
Not knowing what I can be
Always unsure
Not sure if I should be dissatisfied or content
Mad or sad
Disappointed or proud
Constant
Ongoing fight with myself
Or is it peace?
Always unsure
Who am I really?

I Will Survive

by Phillip Matthews

0–1—I was born prematurely and almost died

2 — diagnosed with autism

3 — Mother married my stepfather

4 — started school

5 — parents adopted a baby girl

6 — started to get in fights and act up in school

7 — see Father on the weekends

8 — played with my German Shepherd, Smokey

9 — learned to ride a bike

10 — rode the Supreme Scream at Knotts Berry Farm

11 — celebrated graduation from elementary school at the pancake factory

11 — felt sad that Smokey the German Shepherd died from food poisoning

12 — gave my little brother a black eye in karate

12 — first time in middle school doing well, having good grades and haven't been acting up

13 — learning new vocabulary, dictionary, and people cursing, had a lightweight body under 100 pounds

14 — vandalized the bus with a pencil sharpening blade. Father ripped my phone in half and threw it

15 — arrested for assaulting a tall kid who was putting wet paper on my head—my rage grew stronger inside me

16 — first trial for assault\battery

16 — took three to six months to decide if I was free or fined

16 — saw my grandpa in a casket sleeping, never waking up, I cried when I saw his face was stone

17 — saw my mom and my father fighting and had to choose whose side to be on. I chose to be with my mother. Also, I might not get my 30k and a house when I turn 18 and father will pass away eventually

17 — feel like I will never see my father again, but I have everyone else in my family to help me

18 — I will graduate

19 — I

20 — will

21 — survive

Pain

by Gabriela Cruz

God, I really hope you understand that I had to make them sins,
But damn, take a look into my eyes.
Can you see all the pain?
Can you really see all them lonely nights I stay crying in my bed?

I stay in the streets trynna find love in all the wrong ways,
I have no father to teach me all them things.
Mom's always working she hardly has time for my little sis and me.
Damn, she barely has time for her own.

And yes, I got big dreams,
And yes, I'm really trynna make out,
And yes, all them messed up thoughts going through my mind,
Damn, I'm on my own.

Untitled by Edwin Lopez

We're Getting There

by Edwin Lopez

The future is here and we know that
We want change and less from the past
But we still are influenced by the past
Nothing wrong with using history to make fewer mistakes but
there are some things we have to cease
To completely unify we must get rid of the hate
To hold all hands and not discriminate
The past is in the past and times have changed
Dilute the thoughts and trends of the past and embrace the
difference
In this generation or the next we all live peacefully
It's possible and we're trying
The norms are slowly being dropped
The birth of difference is here

Odd One Out

by Jaylen Cross

I'm Jaylen Cross, a shy kid who moved from Australia looking for a challenge, something difficult, a pursuit to be better than I was the day before. All my life I've been the odd one out, the only African American in a white school, the Australian kid "with the accent." I've grown to embrace my differences and learned some people will love you for being different and others will try to shoot you down. I've faced the challenges of being different with run-ins with many people, including teachers, during my time in Australia, and those challenges opened my eyes and showed me that sometimes people are jealous. They want what you have and because they can't have it, they'll call you out on it.

I'm 18-years-old, and my experiences have given me character. At times I'm the shy kid and at other times, I'm the loudest in the room. But in the end I'm always the kid from Australia seeking the challenge. In the back of my mind, I just keep trying to impress and give back to those closest to me who have sacrificed for me.

I Just Keep Going

by Angel Saldana

I just keep going without any help
It's always on me to make it right for myself
No matter what comes toward me
It won't be able to make me fall
Because you're gonna need something
Harder than a baseball
To put me on the ground.
Even if I do fail,
I'll always come back stronger
To last a lot longer
And every day I always gain my own
Knowledge
To encourage
My little brother
And sister
So they can gain more brainpower
On what they love most
Up in the West Coast

For I Have Plans to Prosper You

by Silvia Siliezar

i believed in you when death and happiness sounded like
   synonyms
i believed in you when my body wanted to just give in

i believed in you as i handed you my heart
with both hands you strangled it and watched me fall apart

i believe in you still, dear god, and you've failed me till this day
don't you hear me yelling at the top of my lungs, begging you
   to stay

i bet you're looking down at me as I'm kneeling to pray
i bow my head to you, i weep and you softly say,

"for i know the plans i have for you, plans to prosper you and
   not to harm you, plans to give you hope and a future."

I Will See You Tomorrow

By Seth Davidoff

I'm not suicidal
I just don't want to live
It's as simple as that.
And I end up cutting.

People taunt
People tease
People ask "why?"

But they never spare a second
To try and understand

I have problems

But the people who don't understand
Will never understand
Because they don't want to understand.

They ask with the intention to wound.
To open up the cuts they so audaciously question me about
And pour salt into those wounds.

They don't care.
People who care don't ask.
They understand.

And no matter how much I'm hurting on the inside,
I will always spare a second to understand,
I will never stop caring.

I will never stop lending out a hand,
Even if I lose my hand in the process.

At least I left a mark.
A good mark.

Unlike those who don't care.
Unlike those who will never care.
Unlike those who left a mark.
Yes, they left a mark.
But a bad one.

One that lingers in the back of one's mind as they ponder…
"Is tomorrow worth living for?"
But even if tomorrow isn't worth living for,
Someone in it is.
Think of the person you hate most to see hurt.
And if you can't live for yourself,
Live for me.

Because it hurts to hear of the countless people who end their lives,
The countless people who gave up waiting for life to get better
It will get better.
And I will see you tomorrow.

I Am Mike De La Mora's Daughter

by Jessica De La Mora

You know that one girl who swallows all her feelings? That girl who covers her pain with the great smile? The girl who hides in her room or in the bathtub to cry? The one who has to pinch her stomach and cover her mouth so no one can hear that she is crying her soul out? That girl who has no self-esteem or independence?

Well, hello, that's me, Jessica Monique De La Mora. I am 17, born on August 5, 1999. I have a mother and father like any other girl. I was born and raised in Venice, California. My family is from Guadalajara, Mexico. Wouldn't it be nice to say your mother is your best friend and that you are Daddy's little princess? I can only imagine how awesome that would be to say and to mean.

My mother is Esmeralda Jimenez. Don't get me wrong, when I say I can't call her my best friend, I don't mean she isn't great. She is, and I wouldn't ask for another mother. But she isn't my best friend because she's too busy being a mother. I can't seem to build the kind of relationship with her that allows me to go to her with my problems. She misses the positive in what I do and always finds the negative, though she's a wonderful role model. She raised me and my sister, Pricilla, who is 21, all by herself. All our lives, it was my mother who brought us everything we wanted and who tried to do everything she could to keep us happy. She did it because she felt sorry for us and wanted us to be happy. In her beautiful hazel eyes, I see all the pain she has endured—her pain and her anger because my father, Mike De La Mora, has been in and out of prison since he was 17 years old. He left my mother all alone with her two baby girls. He broke his promises that he wouldn't go back to prison, his promises to be out here to help her raise us.

In 2001 my life changed forever on the day the cops took my father away from me and my family. We girls were left fatherless, my mother without a husband. I was only two years old, and Pricilla was six. I have no memory of my father living at home. I don't remember the details of the day they took him away, and I don't know why they did. Everything I write on paper now are the things I've been told, not my memories. Since I was two, I have been fed lie after lie about why my father was taken from me. The first lie I remember was my mom telling me he was taken away because he didn't put on his seatbelt. The last story I was told was finally the truth: that he was taken away for committing armed robbery and violating his probation. My father told me this himself just a year ago, on June 19, 2015. I remember the date because it was Father's Day, and I asked because for the longest time I had wanted to know what really happened. I finally had the guts to ask him.

Along with telling me what he was charged for, he finally told me how many years he has to serve. My father, Mike, the guy who is supposed to be my superhero, was given 21 years. This year I am 17 and going into my senior year in high school. All I ever wanted was for my daddy to watch his little girl walk the stage wearing her graduation gown. All I ever wanted was to hear him cheering my name. For years, my father has told me he was getting out in one more year. Now that I'm older and I can see the picture more clearly, and I'm not afraid to ask questions, I see why he fed me that lie. He did it so that I wouldn't lose faith in him, so that I would still talk to him. He didn't want me to give up on him. He didn't want to lose his little girl.

About a month ago, my cousin Jose, who is 24 years old, was talking to me about my dad. When I asked him if he remembered the day my dad was taken away, he stopped sweeping the floor, looked up and smiled. The expression on his face gave me a glimpse of that day. As he began to tell the story, his movements told me even more. He said he was at my grandma's house, my dad's mother's house. Jose and his sister, Adriana, Pricilla, and my Nina Nelly (Jose's mom) were all there. Jose remembers being upstairs with Adriana in their room when the phone rang. Adriana answered it. It was my dad, and Adriana quickly gave my Nina Nelly the phone. It was a three-way call, Jose remembers. He said he had a bad feeling when he looked at Adriana's face. Then Adriana took the phone downstairs to Pricilla, and she began to talk to him like it was just a regular call. But my dad started apologizing to her, telling her he was going away again, this time for a long time. Pricilla began to cry hysterically, repeating, "No, Daddy, you promised..." and she fell to the ground. Jose says she "went crazy." Adriana grabbed the phone and tried to calm Pricilla down.

After that my dad was on the run for some time. He sneaked into family parties through the back door. Once he stole Jose's bike to take off. Jose remembers waking up the next day and feeling angry because his bike was gone. The cops finally caught up to my dad and he was taken away. It happened in front of my grandma's house. Jose remembers my dad staying calm. All the time he was being handcuffed, he kept up a conversation with my cousins and aunt; he kept smiling, asking how their day was going, telling them he was going to be okay and smiling, saying they wouldn't have to worry anymore. My father was charged for GTA, possession of an illegal weapon, violating probation, and armed robbery. Gang enhancement was added to his sentence.

As I got older, whenever I saw friends and family with their fathers, I cried and wondered where my daddy was. For years I always thought I wasn't good enough to have a father, but my mom used to take me and Pricilla to visit him all the time. All I remember about those visits was my mom being angry and the two of them arguing. But I was young then, and I didn't pay much attention to their arguments. I used to hold my hand against the glass, pretending to hold my daddy's hand, trying to get his attention so they would stop fighting. But after a few years my mom began to give up on my dad, and she took us to visit less and less often. She realized she didn't want us to have that kind of lifestyle—the one that included visits to prison. But she felt guilty not letting us see our father, so she had his sister, my aunt, take us instead. Pricilla had it worse than I did—she was older and more aware of what was going on, and after a while she was angry at the world. She never talked about our dad. She still doesn't. I don't blame her. She saw more than I did, but she holds in all her anger and pain.

In 2008, my mother left my dad. That was the year his mother was dying, so those were dark times. He told me that a lot of crazy things were going through his mind, and often he wanted to give up. But, he said, Pricilla and I kept him going; he said we were what kept him strong. My dad was in prison when both his parents died, and when his brother and his cousin died, too. He was supposed to be at my grandma's funeral, but it became too complicated and expensive. His sisters told him they were willing to pay the expenses to get him there, but he knew they were already paying a lot for the funeral, and he refused their offer. So he wasn't there.

Pricilla stopped talking to my dad a few years ago, but a few months ago I was on the phone with him and I told him I had a surprise for him. I put the phone to Pricilla's ear and made her talk. They both started crying, and I could hear my dad saying over and over and over how sorry he was, and I thought about how before I was always ashamed to talk about my dad, and part of that was because I didn't know much about him. I only remembered seeing him in an orange jumpsuit through a glass window. Whenever my friends asked about him or talked about their dads, I just walked away. As I got older, I started opening up a little, but only to the point of telling people where my dad was. Sometimes I told them why he was in prison and sometimes I mentioned how long he had been gone. But whenever they asked questions, I couldn't answer. Then one day when I was in eleventh grade, my friend Kat told me I should go with her to POPS. POPS stands for Pain of the Prison System, and it's a club at my high school for kids with incarcerated loved ones, kids with problems they don't know how to deal with. The club meets every Wednesday during lunch. They feed you and help you learn how to write out your feelings. Even before

Temptations by Kennedy King

Kat invited me, the smell of the food had been enticing. I always wanted to go in, but I was afraid of being judged or looked at the wrong way until Kat convinced me to go. The moment I walked in, Amy welcomed me in the warmest way; she's the woman who started POPS with her husband, Mr. Danziger, an English teacher at our school. That day Amy introduced herself and made me feel like I was home. After I sat down and listened to other people telling their stories, I knew I was where I was supposed to be. I felt like I had finally found a family. Mr. Danziger gave me a notebook to write poems, my story, or anything I wanted to write, and within a week I'd written two pieces. By the next week I was showing Mr. Danziger my first piece, and he was so happy and willing to help me edit it.

POPS is the reason I am able to open up and talk freely about my dad now. I don't need to cry every time, and lately I have made my dad so proud. My stories were published in a book, and my piece *Fatherless Girl* was read at a show POPS put on; a famous actress read my piece. And then I went to Washington, D.C. where along with 18 other youths who are the children of the incarcerated, we talked to Federal officials about the problems we've gone through. When I first arrived in Washington and met all those other kids, I was hesitant to talk to them; I knew nothing about them. But then I thought about POPS, and I remembered how scared I was at first, and as soon as I started talking to the others, we connected. That first night 16 of us went out to dinner together, and in just a few hours we felt as if we were one big family; we felt as if we'd known each other for a long, long time. The experience is hard to explain, but I know that it's because we children of the incarcerated have so much in common, and I know that it was POPS that made me strong enough to begin to tell my story. I no longer worry about being judged or going through dark times. I know there are people I can reach out to when I feel sad. And I know now that I'm a strong, independent young woman who is going to get somewhere in life. I am going to be someone extraordinary. I am Jessica Monique De La Mora, and I am 17 years old.

Letter to My Three-Year-Old Self

by Jennifer Birstein

Dear 3-year-old self,

I know right now you're very confused and scared. You have no idea what the next years of your life are going to be like. What happened that night was your mom had too much to drink and started throwing plates around the house and threatening to kill your dad. A neighbor overheard and called the police. You don't remember much beyond crawling outside to the driveway and watching the police force your mom into their patrol car. You weren't even aware of your mom's state of mind because you were so young. All you said was, "Where are they taking my mommy?"

A couple of months later you saw your mom again. This time it was in a room where she sat on the other side of the glass. She told you, "Mommy will be home soon, don't worry, baby."

When she came back similar events took place. Some nights it was so bad you went with your dad and sister to sleep in a hotel. You were so confused about why you had to stay at hotels and friends' and families' houses so often. You didn't know why you had to go to the social worker offices where they had to check to make sure you were living in a safe home. You didn't know why you were almost put into a foster home. You didn't know why you woke up in a stranger's home watching your mom insert needles into her body.

Don't worry, because you will grow up to live a happy life. When you're around 10, your mom will move to Texas to stay with your grandma, so you won't have to continue living through her disruptive life. There will be days you will feel sad, angry, and alone, but you will get through it.

Yes, you grew up without a mom on Mother's Day and your graduation, your first time of the month, and when boys break your heart. Those challenges only make you stronger. God gave you this life because you're strong enough to live it. Whenever you see other kids with their moms, don't feel sad because you do not need her.

You will learn to accept the fact that she isn't coming back, but you will still love her. Even when you don't want to see her, read her letters, or answer her calls, remember, she gave you life, and without her you wouldn't be alive. You are the oldest, and you need to help your sister get through this and be there for her. You have to help your dad out because he is raising you guys alone. Just remember to keep your head up and stay strong.

Waste

by Daniel Ortiz

Down on the Bonnie Brae block
Where kids would outline the bodies with white chalk
Sitting on the curb with my friends just having a talk
Eating hot Cheetos and and spicy lollipops
Seeing the OGs pass by with the G walk
Or rolling down Hoover with the hydraulic shocks
Bumbling music and drinking nonstop
With the trunk full of the white stock.

Growing up I wanted the power to have the hood in my hand
And say when to close the lock
Be known as the hood's own John Locke
At the age of 12 when I backed up 18 collecting the taxes,
Going door by door and starting to knock
While the homies behind the gate waiting with the 12-gauge
     shotgun
Had to have the 3 gs by 6 o'clock
With my boy Divix with the extended glock
Calling the OGs hoping they pick up
Before an enemy pulls up
Cause with the 18 jersey all blued up
Back in the 2010s when few really remained

Lord please have mercy on me
I'm looking for a new journey

In the Key of Love

I don't wanna live the rest of my life dirty
And I don't wanna go thirsty

Nowadays the new recruits take this life as game
Wearing skinny jeans and talking hard
But when approached don't rep what they claim
Giving my hood a bad name
Never pull out a whip banging on an enemy while having the
    gun to their head
Or leaving their car burning in flames
While the FBI spy taking a thousand pictures in one frame
Even tho I ain't active to this life no more, I will forever remain
Many know of my loyalty to the hood, love is all I ever gave
The ogs know of the respect I've earned
Cause in the hood there's a point of no return
Robbing people and leaving them with cigarette burns
This life I had to engage and learn
And my family was always concerned
Rolling in a Dodge Dynasty with 3 hub caps
With the Hoover tiny locos with guns on our laps
At a young age smoking, letting time pass
All of us never had a dad
Or learned to be a man
Cause we were raised by single mothers
Or our older brothers doing life

Lord please have mercy on me
I'm looking for a new journey
I don't wanna live the rest of my life dirty
And I don't wanna go thirsty

I hate to think this way but it's what me and Divix talk about
    when he comes to kick it

We the Brave

My living room gets chilly when he enters for a visit
I ask how is it on the other side, is it better than prison?
I hate that I can't see you. We did all this to have money for
    that extra KFC biscuit
Cars, women, cars in our vision
I cry and smoke and while he listens
While I express the real, not like the television
I tell him I rap and Ima get our names out there, it's my mission
Cause he's my brother not from blood or religion
I do my best to keep on my groove in any of the 4 weather
    conditions
This isn't for the hood but I'm making a move for me, it's my
    final decision
I'm not in the healthiest position
I'm rapping cause there's too many wack competition
I just write of shit I've been thru so others can feel and do better
    for a well payed commission
And Ima get my music out there regardless of the industry's
    permission
All this built-in anger got me driven

Lord please have mercy on me
I'm looking for a new journey
I don't wanna live the rest of my life dirty
And I don't wanna go thirsty

My real pain I keep it hidden
These words are the door to a better world or admission
Cause from 10 to 16 top ramen soup and drugs been my only
    nutrition
Every move and word is made with precision
Cause any false move throws you down to the bottom of the
    food chain like a rotten chicken

In the Key of Love

Cause all the gangster life was a lie

I watched my boy convulse till he died

I cried till I went blind

Just look into my eyes

I'm real despite what anyone tries to apply

I went from water guns to a chrome trey 57 revolver

Turning 1 into 2, all I wanted was the dollars

If there was a problem my gun was known as a problem solver

I had little stacks but wanted to make them larger

Now that I write I'm planting more rhymes than a farmer

Moving thru pages is a scandal

Like creeping through the night with a candle

But I went from a gangster to a poetic vandal

Aka a published book, Arthur, but you won't find me at Disney
channel

I do it not for my father but my sister, mother, and my brother
who has departed

These words Ima have to conquer

And my pen's a weapon

And my mind is armor.

The Possibilities of Persistence

by Casey Velasquez

What if:

I give suggestions
Request corrections
Move a piece
Or 2

And ask for—
No!
Let's say,
Demand
Election.

Or
You bring your best piece
And I confirm
With a test.

If it works:
I give the go ahead
And you sit satisfied
Or go to bed

Yes.

In the Key of Love

Can we move?
    I prefer we didn't slow down
Now!

Down
Down
Down

In n' Out

Strict left
And right

I don't want to
Fight!
Keep it tight
And this won't become
Something
Where neither learns
The Practice.

Act this way
And I won't have this
Asshole FACE
So often!

Soften
Soften!
S-O-F-I-N...

Or
Whatever,
Let's not spend too much time on this:

If the rhyme
Isn't in line

And consistent
We don't need to request
Assistance
Every two minutes...

right?
R-I-G-H-T
Nice.

Now
Back to you,

My assistant
With persistence
I request [*demand* ;)]
A small amount
Of
   Patience

You're late!

And still
I wish
That you would wait,
Ok?

Let's *play*
>:)

Inside by Kyra Hill

~ Part 3 ~

Who We Are and Where We Are From

What happens when people open their hearts?
They get better.

Haruki Murakami

Two

By Nelson Mendez

Black Hole

I come from a quiet lonely place
A place where someone comes in but doesn't come out
A place that has no feelings whatsoever
A place that reflects your worst instead of your best
Where negativity strives and positivity flourishes
Yeah, I know I'm worn out, but I don't need to be fixed.
I just need to feel loved.

Home Sweet Home

I come from a loving home
A home where happiness is key
A home where there's ups and downs
A home where no one is perfect
Where one day I'll no longer be there
This is a place where family is.

I'm From

by Leslie Cortez

I'm from high school sweethearts
I'm from a toxic relationship
I'm from jumping borders
I'm from two different families
I'm from a family of screams and punches
I'm from another family that's picture perfect
I'm from assumptions and struggles
I'm from giving up
I'm from regret
I'm from dropouts and minimum wage
I'm from immaturity
I'm from manipulation
I'm from insecurity
I'm from judgment and manipulation
I'm from tears and deceit
I'm from fighting
I'm from anger
I'm from hatred
I am strong and determined

My Childhood City

by George Martinez

When I tell people about my childhood and the city that I grew up in their reactions are usually cupping their faces and start showering me with questions. What happened within the walls of my home didn't really affect me that much because I thought that was just the way people lived. Obviously I was wrong. People point fingers at my city calling it dangerous and dirty, but is it really? I never saw it that way because it was my home, I was so accustomed to the environment that I, again, just thought that's how people lived. I miss my old neighborhood of West Los Angeles, my everything resides there, but I guess I had to abandon it for something better.

Photo by Ellie Perez Sanchez

I Cannot Say

by Anonymous

Hi.
My name is … well, I cannot say,
But I am your average girl
And I want to tell you about my world.
Three sentences to describe me.
I sometimes want to die.
And wave goodbye.
Although I am too good to die,
I will survive.

Blindfolded by Kennedy King

Ocean Breeze

by Daniel Ortiz

I feel the ocean breeze
Kicking back and smoking bomb tree
Thinking of this world as a killing disease
Like the air for the Japanese
I know I got no school degree
Not middle or even elementary
But f--- it, I'm doing just fine eating seeds
My mom saying don't leave mi hijo, please
With all due respect, f--- that, I don't owe any fees
I never had to beg on my knees
I only have to worry about my car keys
Money ain't nothing but cheese
It comes and goes, it's not hard to seize
Gang banging and slanging been my only expertise
Drinking 40s on each side of the 7 seas
This life I lead
No 1 has ever agreed
Because heaven is not destined to be
But better believe, even a master's degree
In this world don't mean a job is guaranteed
So I say f__ that and enjoy a malt liquor squeeze
While kicking it at the beach seeing pretty foreign girls acting a
    tease
And my homie on the side doing nothing but burpees
Cause we have to be in shape to protect the E

The beach is the only time we leave our poverty
When we have extra change we take our chances on lottery
8lest ain't Divix, but he's still a brother to me
He's the same real gangster quality
Always has the nose candy that got us in high velocity
And I say this with all my generosity
And the little bit in me left that has honestly
When we buy a pipe we ask what's the return policy
Cause in the ghetto by the sea
Where you inhale gunpowder debris
And see flowers and picture of fallen Gs
I know it's hard to believe

So I take drugs as an escape and relieve
Cause I come from a broken home
Even though I still hold my own
Taking shots of patron
Next day get headaches to the dome
Get up take a shower slick my hair back with my comb
Get dressed and put on my cologne
Walk out and see my homie polishing his chrome
Headed to the Number One Culver City bus always alone
Walking with my broken knuckle bones
I think to myself how my mind has grown
That this life has been the best loan
Telling myself it's just matter of time to get back on the throne
Get on the bus and start wondering
Each line I write got me clustering
I get off at Venice Circle
Hearing foreigners bumping hood music, I guess we're universal
Heading to the beach smoking my herbal
When it hits me I feel like a turtle

In the Key of Love

Writing in my journal
On the boardwalk and see other writers who went commercial
They're fake, I can see thru them like a thermal
They think they're big but they ain't sh--_like squirtle
But I came for the breeze
Looking at the sunset leave
Letting my mind finally ease
Asking the Lord will I succeed
I always followed, for once will I lead
Will others agree
Can my family not worry
One day will I need an attorney
Will my greed and me finally meet
I don't know but for now I'm enjoying the ocean breeze.

Perfectly Imperfect

by Ellie Perez Sanchez

I come from battles and trials
I come from scarcity
I come from a dark past but where
I come from does not affect my present

I might see me as quiet, talented, happy or sometimes serious,
but never sad

My family see me as "the outstanding one," "the one who never
gives up" and as the "perfectionist" just because I try my best for
something to come out as good as I had planned.

When strangers connect with me for the first time, they say I am
a person who everyone would love to have as a friend, but as
they become my friends, they say I am a boring and a religious
person just because I don't do or say the things they do or say

But nobody knows me the way God or I know myself,
I ain't no religious, I'm just trying to change society
I ain't no perfectionist because nobody's perfect

But I identify myself as strong and happy even if the pain
bothers me, intelligent, talkative, and
Perfectly Imperfect.

I am Human
I come from making mistakes too.

I Come From

by the Students of Steelton Highspire POPS Club

I come from the country
   I come from a black dad
I come from a child's nightmares
      I come from Happiness
      I come from Depression
I come from the mall and I'm broke
      I come from a mixed mom
      I come from the 6th grade
      I come from games
      I come from my house
I come from driving around someone who lost their license to DUI
      I come from Jesus
      I come from the sun's flares
      I come from the womb
      I come from air
      I come from a dirty house
      I come from Easter Island
I come from a family with a lot of problems
      I come from the ocean
      I come from SAO
      I come from candy
I come from Harrisburg, PA
      I come from hard times
      I come from crippled people
      I come from dreams
            I come from love.
                  I come from dreams

Drawing by Danaeisha Cuff

False Judgment

by Kayla Hill

Judgment consumes the room
Cuts the supply of air
Lungs left gasping and
I'm left wheezing.
My brain begins to spin
My knees begin to quake
I swear you could hear my stuttering knee caps clank
As I try to attempt to walk with confidence.
Confidence that is reduced to nothing.
Eyes that hold such disgust.
Such judgment acts as knives
As they pierce my heart,
They pierce my soul.
They pierce my mind
Yet I continue to walk knowing what I know
Them knowing what they think they know.
Left feeling the heaviest burden I've ever been
Forced to bear—just because of one stupid mistake.

Love and Faith

by Angel Saldana

Love and faith
Are the two things that give me strength,
It makes me feel blessed
On what I do best
So I can impress
My main ones around me
Show off my abilities
In the same vicinity.
If I fall, I'll always come back stronger
To last a lot longer
And every day I gain my own knowledge
To encourage my little brother and sister
On what they love most
Up on the west coast
To be a motivation
So I can offer appreciation
For people to think of me in a good way
Just like we did with JFK.

I Come From...

by Monserrat Hernandez

I come from the world
I come from a loud community
I come from hard working and loving parents
I come from supportive friends
I come from high expectations

But I also come from sadness and depression

I come from mixed feelings
I come from deep thoughts at night
I come from unknown surroundings
I come from confusion
I come from being misunderstood
I come from repairing myself when I'm broken
I come from struggles I put myself through
I come from letting things or people go that hurt me
I come from creating memories that will heal me
I come from not knowing where I belong
I come from not knowing what will become of me
I come from a war of arguments
I come from feeling alone and empty
I come from the fear of losing people who matter most
I come from the fear of being left behind, forgotten, and
    abandoned

Sometimes

by Cesar Urena

Sometimes I feel like giving up on football
Sometimes I wonder is it's worth it
Did I go through all the practices and weightlifting just to give up?
Will I be able to play football at the next level?
Only six feet, 255 pounds.
I want to help my parents by not making them pay for my
    college education
My last year of high school football is right around the corner
Stressing myself by trying to be good enough to get a
    scholarship while working a part-time job
I am more focused on getting a getting a scholarship than I am
    on having fun playing this game.

Through Me

by Anonymous

I feel like I'm trapped in a clear bubble that nobody sees. My feelings go around like buzzing bees. I wish I was still in fifth grade where everything I felt would fade. I cry and I cry, but it won't go away, this feeling always finds a way to stay. You see right through me, if only you knew how much it hurts me. I want to forget you. And I wish I'd never met you. But you're a big part of me now. And shape who I am today.

The Book They Never Read

by Kevin Fleming

The book they never read
Is about life
About a black king
And about what he liked.
I try to tell them to read it
But it just don't get them hype.
But the book about lies
Is the one that get them right.
And they will never understand
What the king was about
And they will never understand
The words out of his mouth.
My name is un-owned
And yes I might be unknown
But I will never give up
And I sure won't fold.
My music keeps growing
Like a house filled with mold
And my money will get longer
Like the yellow brick road.
Have my closest friends follow me
Everywhere I go
And then that green I make
Will get me some gold
Like leprechaun in the hood, end of the rainbow.

Where I'm from It's Madness

by Marcel Manson

Where I'm from it's madness
Police take you to the station, now interrogation
We in the little room having a conversation
They want me to tell on my brother
But I was taught by my mother never to snitch on a brother

Growing up most kids were taught the ABCs
I was taught to kill and leave the scene vacant
Living in a house that sold crack in the basement, I had to
   embrace it
Money so close I could almost taste it
I remember when they took my mom to jail
We tried to get her out of the cell
But the judge held the bail

Writing raps in Mr. Danziger's class, I call it Show and Tell
My story to most people seem like hell
But first of the month I was hungry, looking for that mail
People tell me to write a rap, but I just write my life
All this in me is a wound, let me get a knife
When police mess with me I tell them, "Get a life."
The only person I trust is Jesus Christ

I've been hungry, remember having no food
So I stole out the store, what was I supposed to do?
One question, what would you do?
Shootout at my house, next day went to school
Like everything was cool, but it wasn't

I was taught to never turn down nothing
And that if you're about the BS, leave you outside like a Hallow-
    een pumpkin
The raps that I spit are so heaven-sent
If the world is not racist, then how is Trump president?

He trying to send Mexicans out of their residence
But if you Mexican, you my family, so I ain't stressing it
Police pull up and treat us like we criminals, like we not human,
Like back in the days of President Truman

I'm from a place where if you not from there, we shooting
And you'll never see a white move in
Everyone in the neighborhood grooving,
I'm the winner of my town, never losing
Wealthy black man in his car just cruising
Police don't think it's his, they want it proven

This is for my peers in POPS
For listening to my story of my years with the cops
You guys are my family, I will never switch
And if I make money off rapping, POPS is gonna be rich

Street Light by Ellie Perez Sanchez

I'm Not Mad

by Emily Kuhlmann

I'm not mad. I know what you did wasn't entirely your fault. We had no way of knowing you were actually bipolar after you'd been diagnosed with depression. Not like the medication made any difference though, you got hooked on that bottle. Just like your father was hooked. But you stopped taking your meds at the same time. We found that out after you were gone. I'm not mad you landed in jail twice in my twenty-three years of life or that the last time was because you flipped a switch on mom, dad and grandma. I wasn't there, but I'm glad I wasn't, or maybe I would still hold a grudge like Dad does. I'm not mad at you anymore; that's all faded to sadness now.

I'm sad that the family I once thought was the closest to perfect is torn apart. I miss having you and the rest of the family spend Christmas morning opening presents or sitting around the dinner table at Thanksgiving with the football game on in the background.

I'm sad that I saw firsthand the venom come from your mouth and attack my mother. The worst memory I have was when you taunted her as she walked by, and how you sang Three Blind Mice because of her poor eyesight. How could you do all of that without batting an eyelash, especially when she was willing to let you come live with us after your five- year sentence in New York, and she had a 10-year-old, your only niece. She isn't blood related to you but she opened her heart to you and tried to help you when you needed family most. Your two other sisters barely helped you. They weren't willing to let you stay with them, probably because they knew what you were like when you were off your medication. But I can't blame you alone for everything since your second to oldest sister fed you with lies because she never liked my mom and was always jealous.

I'm not mad, but I'm still hurting. Hurt because of the betrayal I felt every time I saw the hurt in my mom's eyes, every time you had an episode and attacked her for whatever you felt like yelling at her about that day. I'm hurt because of all the pain and fear I saw in my parents' faces for over a year when I started my senior year of high school. I never wanted to be home because I knew a fight or outburst was bound to happen. I knew you were not okay mentally when you threatened to send me to jail over something so pointless. It was a good thing I was leaving the Valley to attend college in the fall. I wanted to get away so badly. I'm thankful I had softball as my escape from everything going on at home.

It was December 1, 2012. The cops were called to our little quiet little suburban street. Attempted assault. I was later told you were still screaming at my mom as they were putting you in the back of that cop car. What started it all? Because our cat wanted to sit with my mom rather than with you. Now it was the second time you went to jail, except this time you were in California, and you had your maiden name again. I didn't find out about this until two weeks later, ten minutes after I had landed at Burbank Airport for Christmas break after my first semester of college.

I wish you could see the emotional and physical damage you have caused my family. Mom hasn't been the same since. The woman who used to be strong all the time now has moments of weakness, more than I have ever seen since that night. Dad is extra protective of Mom and still holds that grudge, not just at you but at his other siblings for the way they reacted when he had to tell them that you were in jail again.

Isn't holding a grudge a Kuhlmann trait? I still find myself trying to break that habit. And grandma's age has caught up with her, not only physically but mentally. Then there's me. I pray and hope that the mental illness doesn't get passed on to me. I hope never to be in the same mental state you were and are in. I want to make sure my future children never have to witness what I went through as an adolescent.

Five years ago I was in shock when I heard what had happened. That shock turned into anger, and for years I was angry at you for all the pain and suffering you caused us. But that is an old Emily. That Emily didn't know how to forgive. I forgive you now, but I will not allow you back in my life. I don't think I could ever let you back, to be honest.

Now I'm just sad that my family can never be together again. We're just a broken family now.

Teach Me One More Thing

by Katherine Secaida

My dad taught me how to yell and get ready to fight at any time.

My mom taught me never to cry.

My sister taught me not to give a f--- what people have to say.

My mentor, Dana, taught me to appreciate the good in life.

Mariana Hernandez taught me it's okay to cry.

Miranda Hughes held my hand and said, "We can get through anything now."

Linda Duran said, "Love is the strongest drug."

The police taught me to handle my own business by myself.

Daniel A.M. taught me to let go if I want to be happy.

Dom. A.L. showed me how to look at things differently.

Jose A. Pina taught me things do get better in the end.

Carlos Peterson said don't get attached to people, just focus on yourself.

Freshman year taught me how easy it is to have different drugs run through my body at once.

Sophomore year taught me how to be sober.

Junior year taught me to look every driver in the eyes before I get in the car.

Early senior year shaped me into a stronger person.

My body taught me how easy it is to get what I want.

My arms taught me how a hug can make someone feel comfortable.

My voice taught people how to relax.

My feet taught me how to keep my balance.

My eyes taught me how to talk to people without saying one
single word.

My 8-year-old pictures taught me to gain my happiness again.

For the Best

by Emily

I am from Los Angeles, California, born and raised in Culver
City, the community where everyone knows everyone.

As a kid I lived in the best house anyone could have, down
Slauson on Coolidge Avenue, a couple of streets down from
the projects.

My parents didn't think our neighborhood was safe, so we had
to move, and I didn't understand.

But as I got older, I realized the move was for the best, especially
after hearing that my neighbor was shot in her home not
long after we moved away.

Learn

by Milena Mousli

She learned to breathe in a silver city with more cigarette smoke
than oxygen.

She learned to speak in a small apartment on the ninth floor in
the 20th arrondissement of Paris.

She learned how to live two lives when she tried to fit in with all
the other American kids and learned English.

She learned to fit in when she took off her necklace with the
protecting hand that symbolized her Algerian nationality
and tried to learn about Jesus for the school Christmas play.

She learned shame when the airport guards at LAX asked her
grandfather to step to the side for a random check, clasping
his hands behind him as if he were a criminal.

She learned shock when the attacks hit Paris.

She learned fear when she read all the articles blaming what felt
to be her family.

She learned disgrace when she overheard jokes like "That
concert must have been the bomb" a day after the attacks,
jokes told by the same kid who pasted a picture of the
American flag every 9/11.

She learned anger when she heard about her cousins being
harassed on trains, when it was her grandfather and
great-grandfather, along with all the other refugees, who
helped build those railroad tracks.

She realized hate was history.

It had been the history of her family, no matter how hard they
tried to run from it.

She learned strength from her immigrant mother, who wears her
Hamsa necklace every day to work, to buy groceries, to go on
planes, and hardest of all, to drive.

She learned comfort from her biological mother as she held her
in her arms as she cried.

She learned respect from her great-aunt as she heard the
Muslim prayers she recites every morning.

Finally she is learning love

By embracing her history instead of trying to hide it and wrap-
ping it in the American flag.

She has a history.

Dream

by Jordan Lopez

When we were all born and our mother held us in her arms, most of you may not know or have come to realize, but at that very moment when your mother held you, played with your small hands and fingers, rubbed your head, looked at your features to determine whether you looked like her or like your father, stared into your eyes....She had a dream for you!

Do you know what that dream is? I don't and I'm afraid to ask, because in May 2010 I shattered my mother's dream by receiving a very long prison sentence. Once the judge hit the gavel, my mother cried as if I had died. Worst feeling ever. But her dream now is for me to be free, so I will fight my way out.

For those of you who are free, fight to stay out because being in prison hurts those who love you the most. My question to you is: What is your dream? And don't give up until you reach your dream.

Stay motivated!

Put your mind to it!

Be career driven!

Stay positive and optimistic!

You only live once, and you do not want to live it in prison with me.

Follow your dream.

DREAM!

Visiting Day

by John Rodriguez

Drive around and meet those that I consider my extended family. They are happy to meet me, someone who has so been close to the person they love. Do I resemble him, carry glimpses of who he is, bring stories to somehow bring him alive and remind them that he is not in some make believe place, that he is still real? I see it in them. They are happy, but their loved one is not out. They hug me and give thanks, welcome me into their home and near me into the tight-knit relationships, but now I'm on the other end looking in, and I understand how they feel.

We speak of my friend as if he were a figment of the past, recount stories and dig into his childhood like he roamed lifetimes ago. And so it seems. Around the table the coffee is sipped, bread is broken, almost like offerings for the spirits, but my brother is still here and not yet gone. He lives. He is pulled away in a place that I am learning to forget, the customs and thoughts, and I do this without wanting to. But I don't forget him, them, my brothers who are still stuck in time.

And so it is, I have become one on the other end, where normal people don't understand how it feels to love someone in prison.

Star Gazing by Kennedy King

~ Part 4 ~

Understand Us

You're imperfect, and you're wired for struggle,
but you are worthy of love and belonging.

Brené Brown

I Come From

by Aaron Best

I come from depression
I come from rage
I come from anger
I come from hate
I come from exclusion
I come from fighting
I come from not fitting in
I come from crime
I come from jail time
I come from psych wards
I come from expulsion
I come from non-public schools
I come from fighting
I come from risk
I come from having nothing to lose
I come from having no friends
I come from adoption
I come from antisocial
I come from socially awkward
I come from survival
I come from living in lies
I come from being past the point of no return
I come from f---ing society
I come from pro-anarchy
I come from atheism

Understand Us

I come from fading moral codes
I come from you start it, I end it
I come from not giving a f---
I come from insanity
I come from darkness
And this is all that makes me.

All She Ever Wanted

by Crystal Gonzalez

All she ever wanted was for someone to see who she truly was
    and understand her pain
The reasons she did the things she did and hid from the shame

The times she pulled out a knife and put the blades to play
She always felt alone and she has herself to blame

Her nights of tears but she never knew why
Did he forget he made her or did he forget her life?

She felt emptiness that made her run to the pipe
She cried out to God for her restless nights
And still no one knew she had suicide in sight
They misunderstood her every move and disowned her thoughts

Tried to tell her why she does what she does
When her mind held something else in store
But she could never talk about her feelings, so she shut that door

It's hard for her to point out her thoughts are preserving
She wished people saw her differences and understood she was gold
Lord, she felt like cutting when her eyes felt loose
People around her made her feel she had nothing to lose

But a voice told her different
So, she's still persevering
Hoping that one day she won't be grieving

I Question

by Judith Lopez

I question my inability to feel at times
I ask myself if this is normal
If this makes me any less human
Or if this portrays me as a heartless person.
I'm scared to feel,
Because feeling means putting down these walls that I've kept
   up for so long.
These walls that have been up to create countless boundaries
To lock out the people around me.
And those who left it all empty.

Face by Kennedy King

Versatility

by John Bembry

She make me proud, she make me smile.
She brings me up when the world gets me down.
I'm nothing like you, I'm different. She nothing like you, she
   magnificent.
She incredible, she love me better than you. She incredible, she
   love me better than you.
She make me proud, she make me smile.
She brings me up when the world gets me down.
If you only knew, if you could only know.
Keep a smile so the pain it can never show.
Everyone say I'm young but I feel so old.
I don't hang with fake, I rather be alone.
My brother dead, my other brother gone.
Two other brothers changed, the other now at home.
Like the FBI, I'm trying to figure out.
I'm not just anyone I don't chill with many now.
I pulled the scams, I been a goon.
I lost a lot but I got more to lose.
I seen the hate, I made my lane.
They seen me bad, they say I changed.
I was down always down still to make some cash.
Everything not promised, be thankful for what you have.
You was down, I was down, we met up in the class.
I be down, I get you but you never get me back.
Walking earth cold world but we live in hell.

2019 or longer sitting in a cell.

I love her sight, I love her smell.

She worry 'bout me I swear she something else.

Tell everyone how I feel, I don't care 'bout nothing else.

Be real with me, or I'm by myself.

I, me, yes I don't get much sleep.

Mama call me always say she praying over me.

Feel the sides of my past always haunting me.

Warm heart gets cold with a sudden freeze.

"Send a letter soon to y'all, doing a long sentence."

All the pain might go away when the drugs kick in.

Mama call me on the phone say she need some weed.

Everything I been through is why I don't speak.

From the D, to the ING.

They hating me 'cause my versatility.

Sorry

by Jennifer Jasmine Vasqez

I'm not an ordinary girl... I'm unique and different. I'm not someone you can hurt or whose heart you can break because I've been hurt and had my heart broken already. I don't trust anyone, and I barely trust myself. I have trouble making up my mind about who I should and shouldn't trust. I'm an indecisive person, meaning I can't make a decision, or I take too long and don't make one at all. The reason I am indecisive is because I'm afraid to make a mistake or make an incorrect choice. I understand that I'm difficult to understand, and I can't tell you why, but I don't expect you to understand how I am or how I feel.... I'm sorry if I annoy you, I'm sorry if I bother you, I'm sorry for not being perfect, I'm sorry for being who I am, and I'm sorry for being in your life, but I have come to know it's okay to be sorry, but I shouldn't be sorry for being annoying, I shouldn't be sorry for bothering you, I shouldn't be sorry for not being perfect, I shouldn't be sorry for being who I am, and I am especially not sorry for having a life to live for. But just don't assume my life is rainbows and butterflies, because I have my own storms just as you do.

Trapped

by Jazmin Morales

I feel trapped in a dark bubble where nobody will ever see
   inside.
I feel trapped behind this fake smile and the lie of saying I'm
   okay.
I feel trapped by all this work and pressure that can affect my
   future.
I feel as if nobody will ever understand how worried I get.
I feel as if nobody will ever know the true me and how I feel
   about so many things.
I feel trapped in a lie that close friends don't even know the
   truth about.
People always tell me that I'm that happy, cheerful girl.
But I feel trapped in this body that will never be set free.
I feel as if my thoughts and feelings will never be heard.
It's sad because whenever I look in the mirror I always ask
   myself,
"When will my reflection show me who I am inside?"

Nothing Gets In My Way

by Edwin Lopez

You're "ugly."
I'll stomp on you.
Better than me?
I'll still crush you.
Only doing what you're meant to do?
How about your head under my foot?
What you consider normal is horrendous to me.
Me childish? Yeah, right, you're different and that's what I don't
    like.
What do you mean it's not fair?
I defend what's "right."
What do you mean there's no right or wrong?
Stop it or I'll stomp on you too.
Haha, what's wrong? Cat got your tongue?
You were different and now I fixed you.
Now everything is "right."

Introducing Myself

by Angel Harrison

When I get deep into my thoughts and really see a deeper perspective of myself I ask myself that one question: "How do you feel at this point?"

I tell myself as of right now I feel a sense of accomplishment as I have pushed through the hardest and most emotional topic in my life.

Now I wake up and smile and don't even know why, but I know that I'm doing something right. I'm being me, and I won't even apologize for being something so special in the eyes of loved ones.

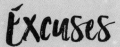

Excuses

by Ana Rodriguez

Miss, I'm sorry I don't have my homework but the smell of stale beer and cigarettes was too much in my apartment last night for me to see the numbers on the page which probably wouldn't make much sense to me even if I could see them.

Miss, no, I don't have my project, I know you gave us a whole month but I didn't know how to ask my parents for the money when I see them counting every cent for the roof over our heads.

Miss, please don't call me out in front of the class for being unprepared, I can't help that even my supplies are hand-me-downs and I'm afraid of being reprimanded for requesting such luxuries.

Miss, I'm sorry I'm late to your class every day.

But the busses come every hour and I swear I run as fast as I can when it just barely passes us by, but the drivers aren't fond of waiting.

Miss, I know I'm the butt of all the jokes, that my clothes fit a little tight and that my shoes have holes in them, but don't mistake me for the school's charity case.

I am not here to make the PTA pout their lips and look down at me as they marvel at my poor little family. I am not here to accept any handouts or receive any pity. That is not why my family left everything they knew in the only country they ever called home.

No, they did it for a chance at a better life a responsibility that rests on my shoulders so I would really appreciate it if you could continue on with the lesson and leave me alone.

My Dream

("I Am Poem") by Hunter Liang

I am wise
I wonder if I'll go to a good college
I hear a song playing in my head reminding me to stay in
    school
I see a picture of my family smiling at me
I want to make my family and myself proud
I am wise
I pretend that everything is alright
I feel as if I'm waiting for something new to pop in my life
I touch my favorite toy, reminding me who I am
I worry that I'll never be the person I want to be
I cry when I think about my grandpa or my dog
I am wise
I understand life isn't easy
I say I'm going to live to the fullest

On Change

by John Rodriguez

The shoes are stuck there as I stumble
and gather my thoughts, and I'm feeling
around and get a sense of the stares
as they pierce me unknowingly,
attempting to gather a glimpse
of who I am and how I have changed
and am not stretching
out of my clothes as their voices
get low and they reconsider
their love, trust, and even themselves,
because what they see planted
is not one who conforms or is stuck
in a little box
with roots nowhere to grow, and their
head pounds, throbs, and drills at
their insides and tests the very people
they think they are
as they now look at me and begin
to understand and let go of the old
me and see that I am
not the same individual.

Popping

by Daniel Ortiz

Me and the homies ain't stopping
'Cause we heard we're the only 'hood that's popping
Straight bucking
25-to-life ducking
Knocking on God's door
Like the hood's liquor store
Dropping enemies to the floor
Looking like deceased corpses
Mamas crying 'cause they're seen leaving in a body bag and
    hearse
'Cause I have a thirst for blood
'Cause I'm a real LA thug
F****d up my freshman semester
Never less tho
'Cause I'm from Western
Feeling pressure
Gotta get better
'Cause I'm known as the 'hood professor
Gotta stay sequestered

Smoking weed and making music it's how we do it
Verbally and mentally hater can't step to me
So they hatin' on me, trying to bust on a g

Ima voice on the ghetto
Where dead bodies make up

In the Key of **Love**

My meadow
Civilians rolling with *stelleros*
Cause we're all *callejeros*
At the age of 16
Sippin' on codeine
But never was a fiend
I don't bang 'cause it's for youngsters
Now I'm a money-making hustler
With my roll dog Alan
Pounding gallons
Cause we really got the street talent
We never had it
Never born with a silver spoon
So I had to fend for myself with my gun tools

Smoking weed and making music it's how we do it
Verbally and mentally haters can't step to me
So they hatin' on me trying to bust on a g

I was never cruel
So had to study and go to school
I was known as the brown fool
I was lost like Blue's Clues
I learned dancing with the devil
Will last forever
I live through the rainy days
'Cause I live day by day
Lived through 'hood struggles
So had to smuggle
To help my mother
'Cause I grew up without a father
And I didn't stutter
It's alright though

'Cause without you I learned hurt
And pain
But I earned the respect you never gave

Smoking weed and making music it's how we do it
Verbally and mentally haters can't step to me
So they hatin' on me trying to bust on a g

Saying we're crossing borders
Borders crossed us nada man
Saying we're not good enough
The system got my homies
Distances
So I speak and you better listen, this is real gangster poetry
Looking at a dead end street.

We Need Love

by Jennifer Birstein

We need love
Even if you're a thug
We live in a world full of hate
Too much anger and violence this is not up for debate
The cure to world peace is love
Love yourself, your family, neighbors and the man above
If we all just spread it around
With no doubt happiness will be found
To Baby on the corner of Fig
Stop opening your legs for $ to these men
To my friend with the gun, put your hands down
Stop throwing up signs and playing around
A life isn't something to play with
I don't care if he missed his payment
To Mama chugging on that yack
Put down the bottle if it's love that you lack
Love comes from inside of our souls
Stop trying to remove an emotion that can fill you whole
When somebody hurts you don't get even
Forgive them and show them some love because the ones who
    hurt are the ones who need it
As the Bible says, be strong and let all you do be done with love

I Am A Clock

by Mireya Sanchez Annabali

I am a clock set on self-destruct,
Yet again I am hidden, stuck behind walls that have been
  rebuilt to keep me safe,
I am the only one left standing,
Yet I am standing in my own way
I am my greatest enemy, continuously making mistakes,
I am the finger looking to point and blame others for all my
  pain, but it never goes away
I am mad, furiously upset, expansion of burning sensations are
  growing in my chest,
I was deluded from heart swaying illusions,
I couldn't see that the large sea was only a dream,
Now, I am awake and alone,
I am drowning and scared,
I am filled with despair,
I am disappointed in my disappointment,
Yet again, I am my worst judge,
I am the reputation that never ends,
My reinvigoration will have to start again.

Painting by Lucy Rodriguez

~⁀ Part 5 ⁀~

Mothers & Fathers

In every conceivable manner,
the family is a link to our past.
bridge to our future.

Alex Haley

121

It'll Never Be the Same

by Alexandria Baiz

I guess I don't know what it means for "it to be the same."

I grew up knowing my father through letters and that one
birthday party he got to attend before going back

As I child, I felt like my innocence was taken

At five years old, during winter break when everyone else was
going to Big Bear

I was going to state prison to visit my dad, picking out specific
clothing—nothing red, blue or tight

I grew up fast, very fast.

With a mother doing everything on her own, going back to
school at night to get a better job to feed me and my three
siblings

Then, when the world decided getting a degree as a paralegal
at 30 wasn't enough, she went back to her low paying job at
the printing company.

I never understood the significance of what it meant for my
father to be in prison until I was older and saw the effects.

A young, independent and scared nine-year-old was what I was
when my dad came home.

He came home with tattoos on his eyes, neck and arms.

These tattoos were nothing I had not already seen on him,
but seeing them in the midst of a family-oriented city was
different

I was ashamed, in a sense, to call him my father

My friends never met him until years later.

He came home, and he was my father, but I did not know him, I
    just felt anger towards him.
It took me a long time to accept who he was and to forgive him.
He did everything in his power to change.
To this day I see it
In the scab wounds
In the fear in his eyes when he talks about it
In the way he gets angry
In the way he lets pride get the best of him
This is why he'll never be the same.
Many things draw me to point to what made him like this and
    what made it unfair for me, my mom and everyone else to
    be affected by this.
I don't have an answer.
There is no answer.
I just know it'll never be the same, and I'll never know what
    "the same" is.

I Was Born to Love You

by Leslie Mateos

I was born to love you. I don't care what people say.

You are my father; you are everything in my life.

For years we spent time together as father and daughter, and
those times in my life were the best.

I write this to tell you I love you and that without you in my life,
I feel as if I'm dead.

Away from you I am now, and my heart misses you and that's
why I cry.

I know the same thing happens to you every day and every
hour

Waiting for my return, I know you're alone.

Rumors have come telling me you have forgotten me.

They tell me you have found someone else, but I know they're
all lies.

People just talk to hurt us.

All they say about you is a hoax.

Even though they say you are not a good man I was born to
love you.

I know you're in a small village, but it feels like hell.

F__k all the rumors of all those cowardly people.

It makes my heart burn with anger when I hear them talk about
you.

Those people don't understand the reason you're there.

People murmur that you are not sincere, that my love you do
not deserve.

If they really knew you, I know they would think otherwise.

But unfortunately that gossip is like food over there in your
neighborhood.

People don't understand how deep our love is.

You are like the cross to my rosary, the hours to my clock, the
days to my calendar.

If loving you is a sin, then my punishment shall come.

May God witness this great love I have for you.

I don't care about the rumors; you are my friend, my father.

I was born to love you.

Dear Mama

by Jennifer Birstein

Dear Mama,

I got to see you before Christmas and you are finally out
I hope it stays that way and you don't go wondering about
I hope you get a job and stay on your grind
Just remember you're always on my mind
Even though you've caused so much pain in my past
I hope this time you're out and it lasts
You look weaker every time I see you
I hope you stay sober and true to your word
"I've changed. I'm not going back, baby, you heard me?"
Yes, I heard you, but it's actions that matter, not what you say
'Cause last time you said that you were back in jail the next day
Maybe God's finally going to answer our prayers
Now that I think about it, 15 years without my mom wasn't fair
But it was all for a reason
That's what my dad says, but I don't believe him
Anyway, I love you and I hope you stay in the clear
And make 2018 a better year.

Parental Sky

by George Martinez

The moon and sun were like your parents since the start
As much as you ignored them they were still there for you
As much as you disliked them they still made you do what you
were told
Warm touches and cold kisses is all it takes to make you feel
protected
Why take them for granted when all they wanted to do was
motivate you?
They are your guardians
You can hide in the night and shift during the day
They're drifting every minute without a thought
Wave the sun and moon goodbye because they soon will have
one last glance upon your face, someday soon.

A Girl with No Title

by Tyanni Gomez

He knows my name but not my title.

His eyes raise.

His face gets red.

I see his teeth, his wide mouth.

The words come out of his mouth. Such hate and dishonor.

"Get out," "You are worthless," "What the f--- did you just say?"

I stay quiet. Shhh…

He knows my name but not my title.

He lifts his weapon, the one he carries, looks at me and says,
    "Shhh…."

What I don't say will show on my face and reveal what happened.

He stops.

He knows my name but not my title.

We walk inside these white walls as if we are criminals

But I'm the one who is accused and is innocent.

I look around my cell and, "Shhh," make sure he doesn't wake,

Doesn't peek or sneak when I'm on the loose.

He catches me and my body boils up through my veins. So I speak:

"I'm tired of you winning, you are no winner. You are no man.
    You are a man who hates and dishonors his own family
    inside these white walls.

You have a lifting power in your body. Your hand, sir. I as a
    woman shall not be hurt by just power. I as a woman will
    never let this happen. I as a woman will stand."

He comes toward me with such anger, I prepare for the worst.

Fathers & Mothers

Shhhh...
Should I shush my loud words?
He lifts his weapon and stops...
He knows my name but not my title
I know his name and I know his title: Father.
He knows my name but not my title... I'm your daughter.

In the Room by Chris Wright

Forgotten

by Leahnora Castillo

18. Who is Dad?
17. Found out Dad was raised in Venice like me...
16. Forgot about Dad.
15. Tried to contact Dad for a little money for Mom and to see if he's changed... he hasn't.
14. Found out Dad has been on the run.
13. Forgot about Dad.
12. Got arrested for the first time and Mom called Dad for help.
11. Forgot about Dad.
10. Forgot about Dad.
9. Dad showed up to my recital unexpected causing my parents to fight.
8. The beginning of wanting nothing to do with Dad in my life.
7. Dad bought me a pitbull for Christmas.
6. First and last time Dad signed a Parent Permission slip.
5. Mom had her 5th miscarriage by Dad.
4. Parents finally divorced.
3. Mom took me to Disneyland in the middle of the night to escape from Dad.
2. My stepbrother called the cops on Dad for beating Mom.
1. Dad was cheating on Mom while she struggled to raise me.
0. Dad wanted Mom to have an abortion.

Even When We're Apart

by Jennifer Birstein

Three years old I could barely even walk as I crawled outside
I heard an unfamiliar voice talking.
Why is my mommy in that car with flashing lights?
She was handcuffed and lost all her rights.
At the time I was so confused about where she went.
So many birthdays without her I spent
All these visits to an unfamiliar room with my mom on the
    other side of the glass, alone.
Only way I could hear her was if I picked up the phone.
By 10 I started understanding my mom wasn't coming back.
Advice and guidance from a mother was something I lacked.
Whenever she was out it didn't last very long
Before she continued to do something wrong.
She missed 16 years of my life and counting
Sometimes when she calls all I want is for her to hear me shouting.
No matter how much I pray
It feels like she's being even more pushed away.
It breaks my family's and my heart,
But she was never there for me from the start.
Every time she sees me, she starts to cry
Telling me she'll change, but I know it's all a lie
There are nights I wonder why she lives this lifestyle
I wonder if my dad saw this coming when she walked down the aisle
She'll always have a place in my heart
I've gotten used to loving her even when we're apart.

When Is It Enough?

by Edwin Lopez

Father is happy, Mother is hard-working, and then there are
their naïve children.
All started by Father and ended by Mother.
Father picked up the bottle and never dropped it.
But it's okay. We're having a good time.
One drunk father and his happy family.
Father picks up another bottle and never drops it.
Father wants more and more.
His addiction got to the point where he took money from Mother
and forgot about us.
Left alone and confused, Mother comes home, cares for us.
One angry mother and her two scared children.
Father says sorry but Mother can't forgive him.
Father picks up another bottle and never drops it.
The tipping point is close but there's still…hope?
I can live in my fantasies but reality trumps.
The man in black takes Father away.
We can't see him. Why can't we see him?
Mother bails father out and it becomes a game of cat and mouse.
It gets violent, all I can do is watch and cry.
Too young to process my surroundings, I ask why?
Why is Father so obsessed with these bottles?
Bottles scattered and unguarded, I take a sip.
It only leaves me with more questions than answers.
Father picks up another bottle and never drops it.

Were our tears not enough? Did we even matter to you?
Out of our lives and far away.
One mother and her children.

You'll Regret

by Solana Palma

I can only imagine what you're like.
What you look like—how you talk.
It took you 16 years to finally write me my first letter.
When I opened it, it looked like my handwriting.
Guess I must've gotten that from you.
I'll never fully understand why you wouldn't want to be a part
   of your daughter's life.
You broke my heart before anyone else ever had the chance to.
But, it's okay.
I don't need you in my life.
You'll regret not being able to see me grow into the amazing
   woman I'm becoming.
You'll regret the holidays.
You'll regret not having the chance to walk me down the aisle.
You'll regret all of your life's decisions.
But, by then it'll be too late.
I am a fatherless daughter who survived your failures.

Pain is Love

by Holland Capps

I lie there on the cold linoleum floor
In a fetal position I stay praying to God for it to end
Her rage floats in the eminence of the hollow house and her
   bawls made the walls shake
I watch muted as she paces back and forth, knife in hand and
   wrath on her mind
Her footsteps echo louder and louder in my head as she
   approaches
I shut my eyes tight,
hoping,
praying for this to be another one of my nightmares
But reality hits when she hits.
The question "Why?" bellows in my mind
"What did I do wrong?"
The pain begins to numb like novocaine in my gums
My vision refuses to focus on the terror in front of me
The blade of depression and fear rests at her throat
My consciousness wavers but I can still hear her piercing words
"You care about nothing but yourself. Look what you make me
   do!"
Instinct makes me stop her
The battle begins, the war has been initiated
The smell of vodka on her breath and her red nostrils and eyes
   tell a story with no words
Can I be mad at someone who is also in pain?

Fathers & Mothers

Perhaps my sorrow is irrelevant.
Perhaps this is normal.
Perhaps this is Love, but
Sometimes I wish she was dead.
But who can live with the guilt?
I will tolerate the pain.
I will tolerate the abuse
Because I know no different.
Pain is Love, she told me.

Squeezing My Heart

by Alexis Parish

I've always had this fear of my mother dying. When I was young, I could never tell if she was going to come home or if she was going to stay out and continue her late night rendezvous. She'd shoot dope in the bathroom and drink alcohol until her body went numb. It was her way of coping with the pain that demanded to be felt.

I remember one Christmas years ago, my mom had decorated the whole house from top to bottom with Christmas decorations. I was so excited to finally spend Christmas with her and my brother. I felt that I had finally saved up enough hope to get me through this one day I had with her—this last chance for her to be my mom again. Then the cops came and raided our house. My heart broke. I felt her hands starting to squeeze my fragile heart, draining it of all the hope I had of ever having a normal mother. The longer her drug addiction and criminal life continued, the more her hands would tighten around my heart. It caused a wall the size of the ones she was confined in to be built between us.

For a long time nobody told me she was incarcerated. I went about my life wondering where she was and why when I asked to see her people changed the subject. I never got a call or an explanation, she was just gone, like she had never existed. The only thing reminding me she was still real was the feeling of her hands wrapped around my heart, still squeezing.

It's taken me six years to understand my mother's choices and actions. It's taken me six years to forgive her for hurting my brother and me as children. It's taken me six years to accept that's who she was, and I can't change that. All I can do for myself is acknowledge my pain from the past and accept it as part of who I am. I don't let her actions change me, but I will learn from them and continue to grow as a strong, independent woman, despite the hardships I've been dealt.

Two Parents in the Front Seat

by Milena Mousli

I have this dad, my dad. My dad wasn't meant to be a dad. He didn't know how to love unconditionally or play fair. All he knew was how to put up a glass wall to give me the illusion of a father. That illusion was nothing but a magic trick with an expiration date of August 2017.

I have this mom, my mom. My mom gave up her entire life in another country to be with my dad. My mom wanted kids, more than one, even. When she got her first baby, she tried to fly, only to end up carrying our family on her fragile shoulders as my father weighed her down.

My mom has this car, her car. The car she used to drive away from 17 years of being weighed down. She took me with her and I saw my dad cry on the porch as he watched us leave his weight behind. But she didn't just leave his heavy personality. She left the bed they shared, the weekly family dinners, the late-night arguing, all the fake compromises, and the grass out

front where she put down a baby carrier with a baby girl in it on the second week of February 2001.

My mom has this secret. A secret she avoided to mention to me for 16 years. But when I saw the blond woman with the sweetest smile holding my mother, I understood this secret was well worth it. I'm happy to say it's no longer a secret.

My mom's car has five seats. At first only two seats were being used. My mom would drive me to school, doctors, therapy, music, and friends. It was always just us. Me next to her. Us against the world, or LA traffic, whichever you'd like to imagine. So when I sit in the middle seat of the back of the car, with two car seats beside me filled by two beautiful new brothers, I listen to the sound of my mother's laugh as she steers with one hand and with the other holds the hand of my new stepmom. I've never had two parents in the front seat.

I have this family. This crazy unconventional family that I only got the honor of having right before I turned 16. This family that I have always wanted. This family that I would wish for as I would blow out the candles of every birthday cake ages 0-8. This family where I sit in the middle seat in the back row of the car, and I finally have two parents in the front seat.

Still Wondering

by Allahna Shabaf

I remember when my friend's dad died
We were just in fifth grade
My mom and I went to his funeral
We gave them assistance
In the form of condolences and money
Their divorce was just finalized months before
So, I knew this was hard on my friend
She was a strong girl—looking to be in the police force
So, I never showed pity
Except at the funeral
I knew she would despise if anyone, especially me, treated her
   any different
So, I respected her wishes
And we never talked about it again
Though I do not talk to her anymore since I've moved from that
   town
I still wonder how she got on
Even seven years later.

True Colors Between Personality

by Esmeralda Felipe-Pascual

My hands over my ears,
Tears running down my face
I feel nothing but fear as I
see the man who is supposed to
   be my father figure
painfully turning into a
   criminal.
These memories trigger my
   deepest emotions
but I know that they are only
   temporary.

Photo of Esmeralda

No matter how different the story is
The ending is always the same...
making you the one to blame.
I felt my heart breaking into a million pieces
As we talked on the phone.
I heard your apologies once again behind the glass.
We put our hands against the glass between us.
I am disappointed in you but ashamed of myself
for letting you affect me
But I learned that I shouldn't be defined by my past.
I'm now 16 years old, no longer a little girl behind four walls.

Knock Knock, Who's There?

by Wendy Rodriguez

Dad, who are you?
You're here, you're there
I will never know
I didn't see you much.

When I was a little girl
You would take me to the beach
And we took our own car rides.
Man, I miss the old you.
I only see you through the glass.

To think you showed me
What a man is like.
Why do I need a man in and out of my life?
I already got that from my "dad"
I only see you through the glass.

I was expecting a change
The good you, the "dad" I knew.
I'm slowly giving up.
Dad, where did you go?
I need you the most
I only see you through the glass.

Fathers & Mothers

Months later you're out,
You're home but still the same
Still in the same lane.
How far have I come without you?
No one will know.
I may not understand you, but I respect you
Where do you go next?
I move on with or without you
I want to see you break through the glass.

I shatter into many pieces
Hurting the most
Not knowing where you're going
Hearing a knock on the door
Who would it be
Is it you I can believe?

Closing my eyes
Wondering, will it go away?
I can't do this anymore.
Drifting away
To a happier place I can
come home to.

It by Kennedy King

≪ Part 6 ≪

Heartbreak

You've got to kick at the darkness
'til it bleeds daylight.

Bruce Cockburn

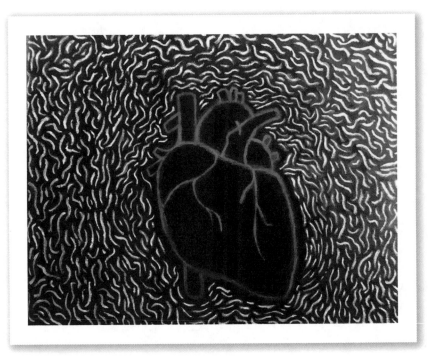

Heart by Nicole Bezerra

Half Empty

by Alicia Valdez

Perhaps the half bottle I gulped
burning the walls of my throat
has blurred my memory, my vision,
the thought of you
but the mere reflection of myself in the bottle
reminds me of the openly lacerated wound I left on your heart,
throbbing,
without a breath of fresh air
for now, I cannot see the floor beneath me
I only see the last drop
calling my tongue's sensations,
the empty bottle before me
wanting to fill the void in which I cannot remember your voice
and the words you used to relax my mind,
your laugh and its never-ending echoes,
or your fingertips and their soft touch sliding down my cheeks,
wiping my tears.

Pulling Strings

by Alicia Valdez

You strum the violin
With immense pressure, beginning to end
Despite the cracks in your fingers from
playing before
The soft tunes bring vibrations to your being
Blood trickles onto your fingers
For you've played the violin quite a while
It is not the first time
You continue to play but you have not noticed the continuous
    drops of heartache from the violin's strings onto the floor
The music makes you sane,
It brings rhythm to your chaotic mind.

Sorry, Wrong Number

by Alicia Valdez

It's 2:01a.m.
my phone is placed on the side of my bed
your number is ready on speed dial, by the number 1
"whenever you need me, you can call me."
I'll always remember that in the back of my mind,
I need you now
I grip my phone shakily,
wondering if you'll ever answer my calls
for I remember
we no longer speak of and to each other
we are just two strangers, ignoring each other's existence once
    again
Who is this?
Your voice, it's in my head
I begin to rewind the tapes of your faintest voice,
the whispers,
the shouts,
telling me you love me.
it's me.
Sorry, you must have the wrong number.
Click.

Countless Nights

by Crystal Gonzalez

Countless nights in state prison, can't break this chain, he just felt overwhelmed.

He destroyed her and didn't even know it.

Those drugs he was lost in allowed her to isolate her world in hopes she could find something he never offered.

She's in love but just wants to see her dad in him.

She misses him, but she never knew him beyond the physical.

She prayed to God for healing but it seemed things were only getting worse.

She broke everything she stood for.

She was numb and nothing made her feel alive.

She lost her mind, heart, and forgot who she was living for.

She became angry and convinced herself it's only God to blame.

She's going psycho.

But, she thinks, no one will drive her insane.

Feckless Tears

by Kyra Hill

I left your eyes weeping.
Red, swollen, and puffy.
You shouldn't cry for me, my child.
I know it is not fair.
I am here for months
While he is here for days
I am here for years
While he is here for months
I am here for life
While he is... released?
I've done petty theft
While he's committed wrongful abuse?
I know it isn't fair, my child.
Know that they may lock me away
And throw away the key but
My spirit will find its way back to you
It will live through you...

Prison Time

by Jules Swales

The last time I saw my husband:
August 12th, the year 2000.
I was ironing his favorite blue shirt.
The day was hot. The sun wrapped
my torso like a cashmere coat.
Afternoon breeze slid
through a casement window,
tickled my back without cooling.
On Friday, August 13th, my favorite day,
he was gone, and I marooned
somewhere between single and widow.

The stranger's voice on the phone
sounded like my husband,
as it carved a canyon
into my afternoon.
I placed the iron down on my hand,
didn't feel the pain as steam hissed,
and sizzled against my flesh.

Listening to the stranger's voice
I glanced out the window
to the vegetable garden
my husband had planted on a whim.
A purple eggplant gazed back.
I didn't want a vegetable garden,

Heartbreak

didn't want a new boat,
didn't want diving equipment
to search the reef for our marriage.

The last time I touched my husband:
August 12th, the year 2000.
We had sex, he went to the beach.
I wished he would have drowned,
or crashed his car, fatally of course.
I didn't so much wish he'd hang himself—
the deliberateness would have been a mess
for my consciousness—

Then the stranger's voice, the iron,
a purple burn to the bone.
My future with no funeral,
no support, no sitting shiva,
no casseroles, no understanding,
no empathy, no flowers,
no sympathy picture next to
    a candle.
No.

My husband was gone, but
    not dead.
I, was burned, but not free.

Half Face by Kennedy King

The White Rose

by Edwin Lopez

I was in the garden looking at the flowers, but you caught my
eyes
I watched you every day—your petals glimmered in the sun-
light, and twinkled in the moonlight.
It was love at first sight.
From the petals to your roots, I fell for you
White Rose.
When I confessed my love for you, you told me "Yes please!"
White Rose—I love you too!
On that day, our journey began
Our new love blossomed in the garden.
You smelled beautiful, I caressed your gentle body
But sometimes your thorns would hurt me.
I asked if I could clip them away
But you told me no
But it's okay, because I'll love you anyway.
We let our love blossom again,
White Rose.
I was prepared to nurture you
I wanted to fight the cold winters for you
So when I asked if I could take you home
And you said "Yes please!"
You gave me high hopes and dreams, my dreams were becom-
ing reality.
Then I realized that I wanted you as my reality

White Rose—I love you too!
All this time I've spent with you, it has been a dream come true.

I've learned so much from you
Love is filled with pain, but it can blossom again
And then we grew our own garden
White Rose.
I was ready to stay with you for the rest of our lives.
I'll nurture you, and I'll fight the cold winters for you.
But then you started getting second doubts
This newborn reality is reverting back into a dream,
White Rose, why are you doing this to me?
Do you even love me?
You told me let our love to wither away, and then the winter came.
White Rose, do you expect me to just watch?
I'll make you mine once again
Let our love blossom once more, and let's grow another garden
White Rose.
Was our love just a fantasy?
Why can't I bring myself to hate you?
You crushed my dreams, but I can't stop loving you.
Why did you stop me, White Rose?
You looked at me with a dying smile
"Young boy, you're too sweet for this world
I love you but I can't let the winter go
It hurts to see you in pain, but you told me that love can
    blossom again.
I'll be here in the spring, but our love won't be the same
I'm sorry, young boy,
There's plenty of flowers out there for you
So please, make your own garden, so that I may see you happy
    again.

Now I must wither away…"
WHITE ROSE!
Even after you chose the winter, I still love you
So when I see you in spring, I hope that you're happy
I only wish the best for you.
         And may the next one be happy too…

Here Comes the Feeling You Thought You'd Forgotten

by Isabella Balbi

Here comes a pang you thought you'd forgotten
Fractions of light that dazzle, kaleidoscopes across an eyelash
    drenched in grief
A chest that's burning and bursting and sinking simultaneously,
    sending ash into the atmosphere, debris across a cloudless
    sky, and cinder blocks into the pit of an abyss
A swallow, an ache
A feeling you can't mistake
The loss of self in a state of melancholy
Turns a person to a wave
Lost in the ether, radiating heart
Turned concave
What could quell this peril?
Perhaps another 20 minutes, perhaps another 20 hours
Enough to return you to the blameless vessel's lot
An eternal sunshine of the spotless mind
Not so eternal, until next time.

I've Cried

by Leslie Mateos

I've cried for love
I've cried of pain
I've cried of sadness
I've cried of happiness
But all those tears were for my old man, my father

A father that had promised me to come back
A father that told me we'd be a family again
A father that told me there would be no barrier in between us
But there was a barrier

A glass wall which didn't allow me to touch him
No hugs and no kisses
No way he could actually feel my pain
My heart racing with happiness when hearing his voice
Even though it was just through the phone

I cried day and night for weeks until falling asleep
I never knew why he was sent away to prison
But people told me it was for his own good
I cried of happiness every time I was told that I'd go visit my dad

Nothing was more satisfying than hearing his voice through the
    phone
Seeing his face while he talked, telling me "I love you, baby girl"
Pretending we were holding hands through that glass wall
Feeling love, pain, sadness, and happiness all at the same time

Heartbreak

Saying goodbye at the end of the visits
Our hands once again supposedly touching through that
  barrier, that glass wall

Chose the Streets Over Me

by Jennifer Birstein

She would rage door to door asking for more of Satan's juice.
She said it made her feel better and got her loose.
She didn't come home until three in the morning.
I'd walk into the kitchen and there she'd be with the bottle, pouring.
From the time I was three, I saw my mama drunk, fighting with my daddy. Some things she did, I wish I could unsee.

One night it got so crazy. She attempted murder.
All Dad wanted was to take the bottle from her.
Neighbors heard us and couldn't sleep,
and then the sirens pulled up, and beep,
They took her away
That was the day

Seeing her put into cuffs pushed me to tears.
Why didn't she see what she was doing to her family?
Why couldn't she stop so we could be together happily?
Why did she have to choose the streets over letting me see her face through the glass?
She'd beg for forgiveness, and I always let her pass.
I had social workers talking to me,
Making sure I had a safe home when she was free.
At school they kept asking why my mom never picked me up.
I told them, "Mind yo business and shut up."
I shouted out to Ms. Garland in third grade for having my back

when the class saw the Mother's Day card I made. It was a picture
of my mom in an orange suit with a bottle of Jack.
All those kids laughed and said I was "wack," but that's just how
I remembered seeing her—either locked up or drunk.
Thirteen years later, and the same thing is going on.
Why couldn't I just have a normal mom?
Now I don't even read her letters or pick up her calls
I'm tired of seeing her go back to her jail cells.

Hate is a strong word, and she is still my mom,
but what she's doing is wrong.
The only thing she ever taught me is what not to do
And that is the thing I know is true.

Childhood

by Milena Mousli

I want to be a child for once.

I was the child of two people with more problems in their brains
than I could count with both hands.
I was the child of two childish people who didn't know love.
I was the child of two people who made sure I knew I would
never be their priority.
I am no longer a child.

I was a child who'd cry herself to sleep, trying to fit my fist in my
mouth to make sure my sobs couldn't escape.
I was a child who hid my pain from the people whose responsibility it was to protect me.
I was a child who would hold back tears as I watched the people
who made me, time after time, leave me on a doorstep like
an unwanted package.
I am no longer a child.

I was a child raised by two loving grandparents.
I was a child who was accepted into a better home.
I was a child whose heroes are my grandparents.
I was a child whose only loving father figure died when I was 13.
I was a child who visited my grandfather's grave every Father's Day.
I am no longer a child.

I was a child of bullying.
I was a child who was neglected until found by some random
adult, with my face bloody and my lungs full of dirt.
I was a child who learned to throw a punch before learning my
multiplication tables.

I am no longer a child.

I was a child who was forced by my doctor to go into treatment
when I was in fourth grade.
I was a child who had to take full control of my treatment in
fourth grade because no one else cared enough.
I was a child who figured in fourth grade that my future was
limited.
I am no longer a child.

I was a child who loved an unborn child more than anything.
I was a child who lost that unborn child very early.
I was a child who got tattoos too young.
I was a child who used every possible escape, from self-harm to
being hooked on drugs to becoming an adrenaline junkie,
just to try to feel okay.
I was a child who ended up being sent away by my guardians,
after talking to my therapist, to a place that had daily,
maybe weekly if we were lucky, body checks.
I am no longer a child.

I wish I had been able to really be a child.
I wish I had been able to be a child whose parents showed up
with camcorders to watch me get something as stupid as an
attendance award.
I wish I had been a child whose only worry was which packet
had a disgusting orange starburst.
I wish I had been a child who had a chance to focus on coloring
inside the lines and the skills to remember the capitals of all
fifty states.
I wish I had been a child who went to Disneyland and summer
camps and nice schools like all the other white kids did.
No matter how badly I want to be that child, I never was, and I
never will be.
Because I am no longer a child.

Party Girl on the Run

by Anonymous

She wants to pop a little pill
Which keeps making her feel so ill
Thinking she wants to have fun
Party girl, always on the run.
This time only time can tell,
If all those drugs killed it
Or, hopefully, she never was inseminated in the first place
Barred from mind that date rape,
'Cause mama's kid's too young to be worrying about a son,
Oh man, what have I done?
She just wanted to pop a little pill
And allow numb feelings to fill,
One white,
Two whites, then another,
Three whites too many
Which had her mind feeling heavy,
Before she knew it, barred from sleep,
Waking up in messy sheets,
Where she didn't know she'd slept,
A big body pressed against her chest
Where her homie used to be, turned into her enemy.

Best Friend by Mireya Sanchez Annabali

Structure by Houses
by Nicole Scott

Big House

I am 18. Biggest and coolest house I've ever lived in. Things get harder for me because my sister and nieces and nephew decide to move away with my mom. Peggy is my biological mother. She writes to me sometimes but she feels as if there is nothing left to write about. I hardly receive her letters because I am rarely home. Talks with my biological uncle to check how Peggy is doing. We make plans to meet up. We do. My little sister meets her mom for the first time when she is 14 years old, like me. I met my mom when I was 14. It was so cool to see her and to see my roots. I'm more comfortable writing her letters than I am visiting her because in person she doesn't talk much. She is very shy and soft spoken when she isn't being shy. We talk about ancestry and I find out that I am Spanish, Irish, and Filipino. We talked about my uncle and how he had a heart attack two days earlier. We talk about my sister and boys. We talk for about an hour led by my adoptive mother and my biological uncle. I can see the resemblance between my sister, my twin brother, and Peggy.

Eastvale House

I am 15. A little smaller than the big house but still a big house. Lots of bike rides here on the weekends when I come to visit from my cousin's house where I stay during the week so that I can still go to Venice during the winter breaks. Letters come every now and then. I sent Peggy maybe one package while she was still in prison. Things are hard on me because I made the choice to stay at my school rather than moving away with my family. I still have my older sister and nieces and nephew. I pick up my nephew from school every day and he stays over until my sister gets off work, which means more time for us to play! Connection with Peggy loses its fire, and we write less and less, my fault. Missing my siblings more and more. I no longer get to come home to them every day. Peggy gets out of prison and goes to rehab

Compton House

I am 13 and 14. In homeschool and develop the greatest relationship with my nephew. Become the favorite auntie by walking with him to the store and taking care of him while my sister goes to work. I start searching "people finder" websites to find out anything I can about Peggy. I find a few names associated with her. I contact Peggy's sister's husband's friend on Facebook which leads me to Peggy's sister's husband and finally, he leads me straight to my biological auntie who tells me all about Peggy, my biological mother, and puts me in contact with her by giving me her inmate number. We talk with so much excitement and I ask so many questions, we talk all day for weeks. I write my first letter to Peggy and wait three weeks for a reply. The first week I think she has forgotten about my siblings and me. The second week I think she is just ignoring us but I am hopeful that she would answer. During the third week Peggy writes back and my mom tells me that it will take time for Peggy to receive my letters. Letters flow back and forth between us constantly, at least once a week.

Gardena House

I am 11 and 12. The search begins and my mom and I start talking to old friends who knew Peggy. No one knows where she's been, they haven't seen her in a while.

Westminster House

I am 10 and 11, wondering and wondering about Peggy, questioning what "I am."

Compton House

I am 9. Forgot all about Peggy, didn't remember who she was or what she did. She didn't really matter at that time.

Ody House

I am too young to remember, unaware of how old I am but I am wondering what happened to Peggy, where did she go, why doesn't she come over anymore, I'm forgetting about her.

Rats House

A time before school, I don't know my exact age. Peggy used to come over all the time and cook for us, bring us clothes, and take care of us whenever she could. I remember these brown lace overalls she got me, I remember her giving them to me and I was so happy.

Loving Eyes

by Shakeenah Cole

Love is blind
Sometimes I don't know what Love provides me.
Love is defenseless
"I'm too overwhelmed to trust you," she says.
Who to cry to, who to laugh with, who to love with...or even
    how to "till death do us part" with.
LOVE
Don't get me started on who I should run away with.
Love is sensitive
Thinking Love, you don't know who you talking to...I'm not the
    one that plays.
But Love, can I talk to you?
I'll cherish my Love if that's ok.

Shattered Glass and Broken Dreams

by K

This is my life in one quick scene. Try to picture it with me, because if you blink you'll miss everything. It's the type of sh-- you only see in movies, so please bear with me.

Shattered glass and broken dreams from being touched as a preteen by that white boy who used to live with me. I never told a soul until one year ago. That sh-- hurt Mama's soul, knowing her baby girl was touched when she was 13 years old.

Shattered glass and broken dreams. Once I was too fat even to look at but then I started blossoming into something, and that's when he thought he had the right to show me these grownup things.

Shattered glass and broken dreams. That's what I see as all this blood runs out of me.

Shattered glass and broken dreams. The pain within me knowing I'll never be clean.

He left me empty, no longer a little girl but a crushed and broken soul being thrown out into the world, and even though he's in the pen, doing 10 to 13, it still frightens me.

Shattered glass and broken dreams now Kametra has gone.

Heartbreak

She is no longer a baby, she felt Ma's rules were unruly and too
    crazy
So she ran away but soon became chained in shackles, a victim
    of slavery
Forced to do tricks for men who wanted to get a late-night kiss.

Ma and me running the streets, wondering where Kametra
    could be,
Getting guns pointed in our faces, telling us we better leave
And they ain't seen no Kametra in these streets.

Shattered glass and broken dreams to nights hearing voices
    screaming
Trying to find someone to reach out a hand and hold me.

Shattered glass and broken dreams, my granny has left me and
    now
My daddy has departed as well, too early
I was supposed to be his princess, his little baby!

Shattered glass and broken dreams.
Shattered glass and broken dreams.
Shattered glass and f---ing broken dreams!

I have so much I can tell you that you possibly would never
    believe
And trust me, this was only half the scene.

On a Wing by Ellie Perez Sanchez

∽੭ Part 7 ੬∽

Looking Back

I can be changed by what happens to me.
But I refuse to be reduced by it.

Maya Angelou

175

Always There

by Kemberlyn Blue

I'm always there, but were you there for me when I wanted to commit suicide?

I'm always there, but were you there for me when my lifeline who was my best friend but he was a dog got taken from me?

I'm always there, but were you there for me when my mom got open heart surgery and I thought she might die?

I'm always there, but were you there for me when I thought I was losing my mind?

I'm always there but were you there when I thought it was me versus the whole world?

I'm always there, but were you there for me when I just wanted to talk to someone?

I'm always there, but were you there for me during all the drama?

I'm always there, but were you there for me when I was here going through it with my family?

I'm always there, but were you there for me when I thought my life was over?

I'm always there, but were you there for me when I was falling off the edge and you saw it?

I'm always there, but were you there for me when I needed a shoulder to cry on?

I'm always there, but were you there for me when I tried to take my life?

I'm always there, but were you there for me when I was fighting with my identity?

I'm always there, but were you there for me when I just needed advice?

Hell, I'd have more reasons, but we ain't got the time, but I was there for you when you so desperately needed me but when it was the other way around, you sat on the sidelines looking at the ground.

Damn now that I realize it, you were never a good friend, but I can't blame you because no one was ever there.

Live Now, Not In the Past

by Jessica De La Mora

I believe in the saying, "Everything happens for a reason." My entire life, I complained about things going wrong and never looked at the great outcomes. I would repeat, "Life sucks, why me?"

But I've begun to notice the smallest things and realize that specific situations happened for a reason, and sooner or later, everything falls into place, everything turns out to be how it is meant to be. I've come to believe we have to keep believing and have faith. We have to learn not to grieve about every situation and that is the key to happiness. You need to remind yourself to be positive and to always keep moving forward. Living in the past can haunt and destroy you. Learn to enjoy every moment in the present, the future is waiting for you. Enjoy every moment in life. You can be gone in the blink of an eye. Most importantly, love yourself.

Live now, not in the past.

Understanding the Seasons

by John Rodriguez

The time when things die down. Plants and animals prepare to wither, salvage their energy and their hope and wait to see if their preparation will last. And if it doesn't, then nobody will notice, because the leaves are not pretty and there is nothing to look up to. Death is equated with life, and from a distance backpacks zip closed, a kid slips on his brother's crisp jeans. The teachers say, "F__k, who will I get this year?"

I sit and think of what could have been, what could have been with the old.... Dwell, sit, feel, and build a love for those who have passed. Skeletons and masks roaming around. I give up a piece of myself for them.

Happy because no longer will my years consists of only a summer and a winter. Away from the desert, from that thing that pulled me in my sleep, made me ache in the bones and challenged me to rot alone, but I did not give in. Learned to love the desert heart. I now love my enemy.

Next autumn, I will take a deep breath and not negate the emotions, those that are good and bad, but sit and remember that my life has begun a new season, with books, love, and a joy for life curled beneath my palm.

Portrait of John Rodriguez
by Mireya Sanchez Annabali

New Chapter

by Jessica De La Mora

High school graduation is the moment we all count down to. Eighteen years sounds like a little until you graduate and see how fast life goes by. Let's not forget our favorite moment, life hitting you. Sounds crazy right? No, it's just reality, it's only been 7 months since I have graduated from Venice High.

Just a year ago, I was a president in POPS the club, getting all my pieces or poetry together for the anthology. Getting ready for graduation, and counting down the days to finally say I made it. It's true what they say, hard work does pay off. If you want something done, you have to do it yourself, it's the best way for something to be done.

Graduation came, I remember how many mixed emotions I had that day. I wanted to shout because of all the joy I had, yet I wanted to cry because of how sad I was. My father wasn't there for another important time in my life. Yet I still held my chin up with all the pride I had because I know I did it for myself, not for anybody else. Am I angry at my father? No, because I know how angry he is already at himself for missing that day and every other day that meant everything to me.

You cannot hold grudges or pain going into the real world. There's no time to sit down and complain about how messed up your life is. You grow up and deal with everything yourself and keep moving onto the next step in life. These past 7 months have been nothing but great and awful to me. I cannot be more grateful for each and every one of those times because they help me grow stronger and more independent.

I Am Just a Minor

by Allan Quintanilla

I am just a minor
I wonder if I could be a writer
I hear gunshots and screeching tires
I see people in the street I admire
I'm a dreamer, not a liar
I'm not the smartest, but I could be an artist
I am just a minor.

I pretend to be an artist
I feel the streets' darkness
I touch my chest, it's heartless
I worry that my love for my mother is not the largest
I never cry, not even for my dearly departed
I'm not the smartest, but I could be an artist
I am just a minor.

I understand I can be such an a-hole
My skin is blanco, but in my roots, soy Guatemalteco
I hope one day I will be set with my own home
Lots of land, a wife and a daughter, yo
I am a minor wondering if I could be a writer
I'm not the smartest, but I could be an artist
I am just a minor.

At 16

by Katherine Secaida

16 I can feel my body full of anger.

16 I can cry like a two-year-old.

16 I lost my virginity.

16 I carried my unborn baby for six weeks and spoke to my baby for one week, crying and throwing up because I was stressed.

16 I refused to let my father back into my life.

16 I already almost lost my life four times.

16 A car pulled up right in front of me and a guy asked for my number, if I had a boyfriend, where I was headed, and hey remember me? I was ready to pull my knife out of my backpack and stab him.

16 I yelled, "What the f__ are you looking at?" Had everyone's eyes on me, I had no fear in attacking.

16 I got two tattoos: "Stay strong" and wanting more.

16 I refuse to give it my all again.

16 I realize that I'm on the moon and no one can knock me down anymore.

Just Chillin' in the Car

by Imari Stevenson

Sometimes I have flashbacks.
Sometimes I feel the pain.
Even though it happened years ago, the pain remains.
One sunny day, I thought it would all be the same.
BOOM!
Like that, everything changed.
A guy came out of the bushes, all buff and frame.
I was sitting in the car with my sister
And there he came
Screaming and yelling and putting fear in my sister's face and mine.
My mom was on the floor, filled with pain.
I felt as if I were the one being thrown away.
My body was frozen. I felt ashamed.
I sat there and cried
And felt my mom was about to die.
I was only 7 or 8 years of age.
Helicopter, police, friends and family approached
The guy ran off
My sister and I got questioned.
He was caught
But the flashbacks remain.

Detained

by John Bembry

They had me detained for wanting the money. *(All in the wood and down here in Venice.)*
I been detained, I'm black, for nothing. *(I'm always plotting, I'm always on missions.)*
My brother detained out of the county. *(From Carson Del Amo to Florida, Tampa.)*
I got detained but then I got lucky. *(Living this life too much stuff will happen.)*

When I make it off of probation, time to get money, no time for vacation. We working and faded. I went through these phases and made all these changes to be able to make it.
My family been through some s___, but none is in vain. I don't have side chicks,
No girl beside me. My girl is money, I made her my main.

I done heard people tell me they gone kill me. I done heard people tell me that I'm switching. Yet I'm still living, you better be cautious. All of that talking, come show me you with it.
Disrespect me, I can't show no feelings. I live the life, I'm not trying to get sentenced.
I hang with people that really get money and really got bodies that mean they some killers.

They had me detained for wanting the money. *(All in the wood and down here in Venice.)*
I been detained, I'm black, for nothing. *(I'm always plotting, I'm always on missions.)*
My brother detained out of the county. *(From Carson Del Amo to Florida, Tampa.)*
I got detained but then I got lucky. *(Living this life too much stuff will happen.)*

I'm glad I didn't go to prison. I left him living, 'cause he got children. I have a future and his is not certain.
He not with his daughter 'cause he got a sentence.
Only the real, always the facts, neck getting cramped, Inglewood on my back.
Put us all on the map. They sad, still doing pills, meth and the crack.
Heard my little brother got caught and detained. Most of the homies got caught and detained. Some went in and come out not acting the same. Still doing drugs and they living in shame.
I made right choices because of the pain! YEA. I'm blessed and destined for all of the fame! YEA.

Two of the homies still caught and detained. Back and forth, in and out at a young age. Contagious, avoiding it like it's the plague. Different designer, I craft and create.
I know some real, I know some fake. I got some love, they got some hate.
Still too slow, I'm at a faster pace. Thinking how they shot you all in the face.
I swear, when I make it off of probation, don't let me see them two faces.
I'm always gone in different places.

Think of my problems it's cases on cases on cases on cases on cases on cases.

Not getting hit with the numbers. Five of mine dead in a slumber. I been the prey, now I'm the hunter.

Living this life, you gone fall but keep going. Homies are dying, the numbers are growing.

Stick to myself and don't show no emotions. Steady the pace, yeah I'm keeping the motion. They had me detained all over the city because my skin black and I found it repulsive.

I'm not religious, I'm living my culture. Yeah it's a lot but I thought you should know it.

They had me detained for wanting the money. *(All in the wood and down here in Venice.)*

I been detained, I'm black, for nothing. *(I'm always plotting, I'm always on missions.)*

My brother detained out of the county. *(From Carson Del Amo to Florida, Tampa.)*

I got detained but then I got lucky. *(Living this life too much stuff will happen.)*

~⊸ Part 8 ⊷~

Six Word Memoirs

It's very hard to put yourself out there, it's very hard to be vulnerable, but those people who do are the dreamers, the thinkers, the creators. They are the magic people of the world.

Amy Poehler

My Fingerprint, by Talaya Manigault

Six Word Memoirs

One day and after enjoying volunteer Claire LaZebnik's home-baked brownies for dessert, two Santa Monica High POPS students were inspired to write these two six word memoirs:

My Brownie
by Pablo Gonzalez

Hypnotic, delicious, fattening, regret, sweating, made it

My Teeth
by Bryce Smith

Unsatisfied, unsure, processing, finished, happy, cautious

Several others in the club decided they wanted to contribute their six word memoirs, too:

Love is trust, companionship, and compassion
by Samaiya Kirby

Holding hands but he's wearing handcuffs.
by Owen Halpert

In the Key of **Love**

Twelve a.m. at the police station.
by Ireland Neville

And the students of El Camino Charter High POPS
were also moved to write a few:

Wanted
Full time
And loving father
by Juan Salas

Can't manage to love you again
It's hard to be myself now
Life is my only true downfall
I hid in my shadows afraid
by Anonymous

Part 9

See Our Stories

Art is not what you see.
but what you make others see.

Edgar Degas

Beautiful by Kennedy King

Johnny Rodriguez by Mireya Sanchez Annabali

John Bembry by Mireya Sanchez Annabali

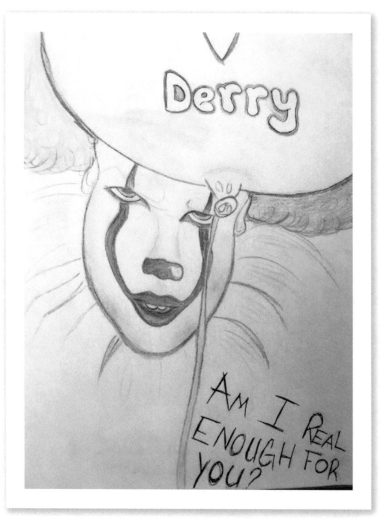

Exaggerated by Kennedy King

Not Yet Perfect by Kennedy King

Drawing by Mireya Sanchez Annabali

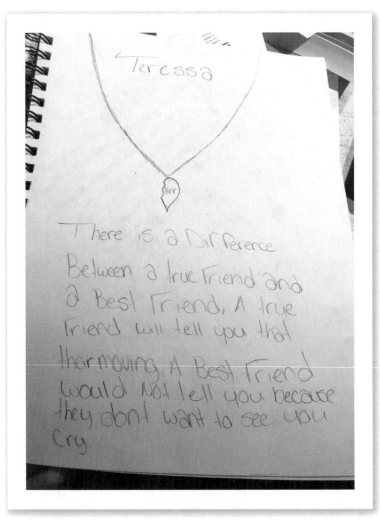

Teressa by Kennedy King

John Rodriguez by Chris Wright

Épilogue

by Claire LaZebnik

Sometimes, when you think you're helping other people, you're really just helping yourself.

That's true for me with volunteering for POPs. It may sound like I'm being unselfish—"I can't have lunch with you on Monday because that's the day I go to Santa Monica High School to help run a lunch club for kids whose lives have been impacted by incarceration"—but the truth is, this organization has done far more for me than I have for it.

It has, for example, introduced me to some of my new favorite people, from my fellow volunteers, who are kind and empathetic, to the teachers at the high school who generously give up their free time to host or visit the club, to the brilliant and passionate people who run POPS.

Another bonus: food is a big part of our lunch club, because nothing conveys warmth, acceptance and welcome like a big plate of deliciousness, and I love to eat. So there's that.

But the real pleasure of volunteering comes from being with these amazing students. Most of them started off shy, slightly wary of strangers bearing free food, but over time, more and more of them have opened up, tentatively telling us about their lives, their hopes, and their fears. Some talk more than others; some hover in corners and barely seem to be paying attention; some expand only to withdraw again, and some only show up occasionally—but every time a kid walks into the room or shares a personal story with us, it feels like a victory, and I realize once again how lucky I am to be a part of this amazing organization, and how glad I am that they are sharing their stories with you.

Acknowledgments

So many people devoted time, energy and talent to make this collection possible—it's impossible to offer sufficient thanks to all of them.

POPS the Club and this anthology would not be possible without the teachers, counselors and volunteers who dedicate themselves to creating sacred space for youth who have struggled with the "Pain of the Prison System."

In LA at Belmont High: Principal Elsa Mendoza, Nora Artine, Nicole Taylor, Daniel Robinson, Jackie Heinze; at Culver City High: Jose Montero, Carlos Valverde, Jackie Beyer, Bianca Lopez, Zoe Garaway, Claire Lazebnik; at El Camino Charter High, James DeLarme, Emily Kuhlmann, Stacey Cohan, Sonia Faye; at James Monroe High, Reggie Quemuel, Thomas Wu, Merrill Markoe, Laurie Sandell, Claudette Sutherland, Matthew Tester; at LA High School of the Arts, Lizzy Mora, Principal Susan Canjura, Casey Velaszquez, Phil America, Carly Beck, Melissa Merritt; at Lawndale High, Michelle Lee, Mir Reza, Tuan Hophan, Jen Turk, Bianca Lopez, Nicole Taylor; at Santa Monica High, Annette Gromala, Shuli Lotan, Claire Lazebnik, Christy Hobart, Victoria Andahazy; at Venice High, Drake Witham, Dennis Danziger, Lucy Rodriguez, Anneke Campbell, Jules Swales, Andrea Blake, Kelly Slattery. In Harrisburg, Pennsylvania at Steelton Highspire High School, Jennifer Morrison, Heather Bobula; at Sci Tech High School, Sunada Roberts, Stacey Rossi and Tiana Reid; in Baltimore, Amy Wilson and Tholyn Twyman, at Renaissance Academy Kaitlyn Rosa, Hallie Atwater; in Atlanta, Georgia, Denise Wright of Atlanta's Communities in Schools, Danielle Whylly, US Attorney's Office at Benjamin E. Mays High School, Mr. Jackson, Courtney Sutton; at G.W. Carver High School, Mr. Simon, Nicole Bush. We thank our hardworking team in NYC, guided by Marianna Houston, Deanna Paul and Anita Pepper, bringing POPS the Club in Fall 2018 to Bronx Academy of Letters, Principal Brandon Cardet-Hernandez, teachers Michael Alston, Karla Rodriguez; at William Cullen Bryant High School, Principal Namita Dwarka, teachers Kelly Gilles, Adam Somer.

Acknowledgments

Deepest gratitude to those who feed us, special gratitude to Fernando Lopez of Guelaguetza, Teri Ernst and Angie Cabrera at Dinah's Family Restaurant, Dave Licht and Silvia Lopez of KayNDaves Cantinas and Steve Cohen of Village Pizzeria.

Our staff is small but mighty, and I want to say special thanks to them for always being there. Thank you Sonia Faye, Deputy Director, Arielle Harris, Volunteer Coordinator and Lauren Marks, Communications Manager.

Oceans of gratitude for their guidance and leadership to our Board of Directors: Dr. Vincenzo Sainato, Chair, Carol F. Burton, Vice Chair, Dennis Danziger, Secretary (and POPS co-founder), Paul Hosch, Treasurer, John Rodriguez, Anastasia Stanecki and Jennifer Turk.

Thank you to mentors Jonathan Zeichner of A Place Called Home and Rachel Davenport, and to Vital Voices Global Ambassadors Program.

And to those who keep our coffers full and the lights on. This volume would never see the light of day if it weren't for The Adams Family Foundation, The California Endowment, Executive Service Corps of Southern California, The Durfee Foundation, The Dwight Stuart Youth Foundation, Trial Lawyer Charities, Judicate West Foundation, The Venice High Alumnae Association, Wes Com's We Care Foundation, Women Helping Youth, Madge Stein Woods and to so many generous, kind and compassionate individuals.

And thank you to our resilient, brave, bold, vibrant and talented students!

Contributor Bios

Mireya Sanchez Annibali is president of POPS Venice High, a writer and an artist graduating in 2018.

Kayla Armstrong is a 17-year-old girl who wants to be an inspiration to young girls and wants them to know that they are not alone in the world and to know that they are beautiful and smart and strong.

Alexandria Baiz is a student at POPS the Club Culver City High.

Isabella Balbi is a senior member of POPS at El Camino Real. She is passionate about social activism and the arts. She hopes to pursue a career in writing after becoming the first college graduate in her family.

John Bembry "The stories I write and the life I live/Was destined to me ever since a Kid In the Squadd/Yet I trust at the Top it's just us/We aren't what we not/One time just for POPS." ~ GodBless

Aaron Best I've been in and out.

Nicole Bezerra I love everything about art, especially how it allows me to express how I feel without words and lets me unwind and take a mini-break from life. I love art that is open for interpretation and I feel my piece in this book is.

Jennifer Birstein is a senior at El Camino Charter High who wants to make a difference in the world and not let anybody feel alone.

Kemberlyn Blue is a student at POPS Culver City High.

Holland Capps is a student at POPS the Club Santa Monica High.

Leahnora Castillo is 18 years old, born and raised in Venice, California. "I love to dance and write."

Shakeenah Cole. I am a young artist and poet from Baltimore. I would like to be a famous artist and poet and to also continue to be a big dreamer.

Leslie Cortez is a 15-year-old Mexican American born in a chaotic area of Los Angeles. She attends Los Angeles High School for the Arts and is determined to be a successful adult in the future.

Jaylen Cross is a student at POPS Culver City High.

Gabriela L. Cruz lives in South Central L.A. She is 15 and she's trying to be a model.

Danaeshia Cuff. I am 14 years old, don't like school and my principal. I like art, drawing and reading. People are boring.

Seth Davidoff is a member of POPS Santa Monica High.

Jessica De La Mora was president of POPS the Club Venice High until her graduation in 2017. She loves to write.

Mya Edwards is a 15-year-old artist and a sophomore at Venice High School.

Esmeralda Felipe-Pascual is a member of the POPS Club at Belmont High in Los Angeles.

Kevin Fleming I think of myself as a king; not just any king, but a young black king. I'm strong, smart, and I don't give up on what I want. Don't tell me the sky is the limit when there's footprints on the moon.

Angela Gomez is a member of POPS the Club.

Tyanni Gomez. My father and I are have been doing well since I graduated a few years ago from Venice High; I am majoring in English & Cybersecurity at Long Beach City College and will join the Air Force after I receive my AA.

Crystal Gonzalez is a POPS Venice student.

Pablo Gonzalez is a POPS Santa Monica High student, who loves brownies.

Owen Halpert is a POPS Santa Monica High student.

Angel Harrison is a student at POPS El Camino Charter High.

Brian Hernandez likes to help people and play sports.

Monserrat Hernandez is a 15-year-old unknown girl in a loud community. She currently attends Los Angeles High School for the Arts (LAHSA) at RFK. She doesn't know yet what she'll expect in life.

Brian Hernandez, a student at Venice High POPS, likes to help people and play sports.

Kyra Hill is a 9th grader at Sci Tech High and a member of Sci Tech's POPS Club.

Kennedy King. I'm 14 years old, live with my mom, dad and three sisters. I love to read, write and draw. (Steelton Highspire)

Samaiya Kirby is a student at POPS Santa Monica High.

Emily Kuhlmann is a volunteer at El Camino Charter High POPS.

Claire LaZebnik is an author and activist serving who volunteers at Santa Monica and Culver POPS clubs and serves as POPS the Club's volunteer liaison.

Hunter Liang is a student at El Camino Charter and a member of the POPS Club there.

Bianca Lopez is a student at West LA College and a volunteer at POPS Lawndale who graduated from Venice in 2015 and continues to be an active member of POPS the Club.

Edwin Lopez is in POPS the Club at James Monroe High, a writer and an artist.

Jordan Lopez is a big fan of POPS. He adores his sisters, Bianca and Daisy, who are longtime members of POPS.

Judith Lopez is a sixteen-year-old who aspires to become an FBI agent.

Talaya Manigault. I'm an African American woman who likes gym, painting and slime.

Marcel Manson plays football at Venice High.

George Martinez is a student at Lawndale High, a member of POPS the Club.

Leslie Mateos graduated from Venice High in 2017 and is attending college.

Phillip Matthews. I am a 17-year-old boy who has a disability and it's autism. Also, I am a positive person, a nerd, and very shy.

Kei'Arri McGruder is a poet who graduated from Venice High in 2017.

Amy Medina enjoys reading and writing poetry.

Nelson Mendez is a 15-year-old sophomore at LAHSA trying to figure out what to do in life.

Milena Mousli is a writer and artist.

Jazmin Morales is a member of POPS El Camino Charter High.

Ireland Neville was one of the first members of POPS Santa Monica High.

Amyas Njoku is a member of POPS the Club at Culver City High.

Daniel Ortiz. Only the scared look over their shoulder.

Solana Palma is the president of Culver City High School's POPS Club.

Alexis Parish is a 16-year-old California native who loves to write and procrastinate.

Ellie Perez Sanchez is a 16-year-old student at Los Angeles High School for the Arts who loves photography and believes we are all perfectly imperfect, but that faith moves mountains.

Allan Quintanilla is a writer and student at Venice High and a member of POPS the Club.

Ana Rodriguez is the president of POPS El Camino Charter High.

John Rodriguez is a writer that will step onto a university campus to pursue English and one day eventually teach in a classroom.

Lucy Rodriguez is an artist, a POPS grad, an ambassador and a volunteer at Venice High.

Wendy Rodriguez is a roller coaster.

Juan Salas is a student at El Camino Charter High Continuation School.

Angel Saldana. My creation is the story that I've made about my lifetime.

Nicole Scott is 18, a writer, a lover.

Katherine Secaida (Kat), a POPS Venice grad and college student reminds others that without the dark, we'd never see the stars.

Allahna Shabaf. I'm a senior at Lawndale High School. I've only been at this school since junior year. I transferred from Renaissance High School of the Arts in Long Beach. My biggest passion is music, which is why I went to Renaissance for the first two years of high school.

Silvia Siliezar is a writer and a senior at Venice High.

Bryce Smith is a student at POPS Santa Monica High.

Imari Stevenson. There is only one race and that is human. We must all stick together through thick and thin.

Jules Swales is a published writer living in Los Angeles. Poetry is her love although she has published non-fiction with a book soon to be released. Jules studied for 12 years with Jack Grapes and runs her own writing/editing groups. She has a love of writing, a love of people and a love of all the twists and turns of life.

Cesar Urena plays football at Venice High.

Alicia Valdez is a junior at Venice High School who continuously seeks laughter even in the most dire situations.

Jennifer Jasmine Vasquez is a member of POPS the Club at Belmont High.

Casey Velasquez is a yoga and mindfulness teacher who volunteers at POPS LAHSA.

Hazel Kight Witham is a poet and an English teacher at Venice High who wrote this poem for all the students of POPS the Club in honor of the club's fifth anniversary.

Chris Wright is an art teacher at Venice High and a long-time POPS supporter.